THE S.E.A. WRITE

THAI SHORT
AND PO_ERMS

EDITED BY

NITAYA MASAVISUT
MATTHEW GROSE

SILKWORM BOOKS
CHIANG MAI

ISBN 974-7100-68-1

First published in 1996, reprinted in 1998 by
Silkworm Books
54/1 Sridonchai Road, Chiang Mai 50100, Thailand
E-mail: silkworm@pobox.com

Design by T. Jittidejarak
Cover photograph by Nibondh Hutintha
Cover graphic by Klik Studio
Set in Garamond 10.5 pt. by Silk Type

Printed in Thailand by O.S. Printing House, Bangkok.

FOREWORD

The short stories and poems represented in this anthology have been selected from the works of eleven contemporary Thai writers and poets whose masterpieces have won the prestigious Southeast Asian Write Award, popularly known as the "S.E.A.Write."

Established in 1979, the award was initiated by the management of the Oriental Hotel. Inspired by its traditional association with world-renowned authors such as Joseph Conrad, Somerset Maugham and Graham Greene, the management of the Oriental Hotel in collaboration with Thai Airways International and several other private organizations decided to launch a literary prize to be awarded annually to outstanding contemporary writers from ASEAN countries. The main objectives are to promote and recognize contemporary writers in the region and to create closer ties among them.

In Thailand the Thai PEN Center and the Writers Association have been responsible for the selection of the prize-winning works. It was decided that only three main genres—novels, poetry, and short stories—would be alternately taken into consideration. In addition to their literary value, the works have been judged on the basis of their originality, creativity, and their contribution to society at large. In all, six novels, six collections of short poems, and five collections of short stories have been awarded this literary prize.

After seventeen years of accomplishment, the James H. W. Thompson Foundation, one of the award's staunch supporters, felt that these Thai contemporary masterpieces should be translated into English so that international readers would be able to appreciate Thai literary works. The Foundation offered to provide the funding for the translation project and asked Thai PEN Center to undertake this ambitious task.

HRH Prince Prem Purachatra, a highly esteemed literary scholar once said that the soul of the people is often revealed in their literature. It is hoped, therefore, that this S.E.A. Write anthology of poems and short stories will give international readers deeper insight into Thai culture and a better understanding of contemporary Thai literature as a whole.

Nitaya Masavisut
President, Thai PEN Center

ACKNOWLEDGMENTS

The Thai PEN Center would like to express its sincere gratitude to the James H. W. Thompson Foundation for the funding of this translation project. Without such generous assistance this S.E.A. Write anthology of short stories and poems would have been impossible. Our heartfelt appreciation goes to all the translators who have given so unsparingly of their expertise and time. Their unremitting enthusiasm and selflessness have encouraged us to go on with this task. For editorial assistance we owe special thanks to Ngarmpun Vejjajiva of Silkroad Publishers Agency. Matthew Gross of Rangsit University did a superb job in reading over the manuscript, editing, and making insightful comments for which we are deeply indebted.

Finally we are most grateful to all S.E.A Write awardees for having been generous in letting us translate their works into English.

International PEN, Thai Center

CONTENTS

CONTENTS

INTRODUCTION

WHEN the S.E.A. Write Award was established in 1979, Thailand had just marked two very significant events; one was the student and populist uprising which toppled the military government in 1973, and the other was the brutal killing of the "leftists" which led to the 1976 coup and the flight to the jungle of student activists and intellectuals.

It is not surprising, therefore, that some of the works included in this anthology should reflect the sentiments arising from these two crucial events. In fact, some writers and poets whose masterpieces have been chosen for this collection were among those who fled to the hills in 1976 and came back after an amnesty was granted in 1978–1979.

The collection of poems, *Mere Movement,* by Naowarat Pongpaiboon, the 1980 S.E.A. Write awardee, clearly reflects these sentiments. Imbued with democratic ideology and emotionally charged by the October 1973 popular and student uprising, Naowarat wrote a revolutionary and prophetic poem, *The Way of the Snail,* in which he encourages the people to be patient and begin to "paint the silver path" which he believes will eventually lead to the ideal society where "the blazing sun will lash out in anger with its rays and consume the weeds' domain". But the people did not have to wait long, because the weeds' domain was consumed right after *The Way of the Snail* was written, and Naowarat celebrated this victory with grace and dignity in his *Mere Movement:*

> A promise astir, of nothing evil
> but of grace, and beauty taking shape.

There amid the stillness murky,
the beginning is begun.

Listen to the temple drums.
Observe another Holy Day.
Hear the booming of the guns
mark the people's battle-cry.

Chiranan Pitpreecha's collection of poems, *The Lost Leaf,* which
won the S.E.A. Write Award in 1989, also reveals the defiant spirit
of its author since she herself was one of the student activists who,
after the October 1973 uprising, became a leader of the women's
liberation movement and finally fled to the hills in 1976. Her
poem, *The Defiance of a Flower*, which was written shortly after
October 1973, can readily serve as a women's declaration of
independence. According to her, women should be respected for
their worth and dignity. They are like flowers with sharp thorns
and are meant for higher things than to slake the lust of men.

Her poem, *Life*, which was written during her armed struggle in
the jungle, is about her own experience of giving birth to her first
child. Here, her defiant spirit has been replaced by one of mother-
hood, which fills her with pride and hope for the future:

The tiny life from within me
Stirs my life with ecstasy
Fills me with happy hope,
With daring delight
And dreams of valour
I who am a mother.

Khomthuan Khanthanu's *Drama on a Wide Arena*, another
collection of poems which won the S.E.A. Write Award in 1983,
also echoes the anger and bitterness felt by young writers of the
October 1976 period. In almost all of the poems in this collection,
he openly attacks the rich and the powerful and accuses them of

causing the suffering of the poor and the underprivileged. This resentment is clearly expressed in his *Beggar's Chant*:

> lazy we were not
> servile we were not
> we tilled and ploughed
> we farmed the land
> and reaped the debts
> the rich are big brothers
> we owe money we are the dogs
> our tongues hang out
> our bellies rumble
> rice farmers begging rice from others
> can anyone understand
> can anyone understand

The prize winning works that have been discussed so far may give international readers the impression that Thai literary works after the 6 October 1976 political upheaval are predominently political. Indeed, these two events of 1973 and 1976 had a significant impact on the young writers who lived through that terrible period. They wrote about their experiences and their resentment of the social and political conditions of the time, but none of their work can be labeled as propaganda. With their original styles and literary techniques they were able to create contemporary works of great literary value.

Many of the short stories in the collection, *Khunthong, You Will Return at Dawn*, by Ussiri Thammachot, the 1981 S.E.A. Write awardee, were also inspired by the two political upheavals. However, his two short stories selected for this anthology are of a different nature. In *Nightfall on the Waterway*, Ussiri deals with an ethical problem by depicting the dilemma of a poor watermelon grower who has to chose between committing a moral crime or bringing happiness to his careworn wife and daughter. Finally, the farmer manages to justify his decision to steal by trying to convince himself that what he is about to do is no crime at all:

After all, he was the discoverer of this treasure, he had gone through the ordeal of fearful lonesomeness with this bloated corpse, he had borne its unbearable stench in this moon-blanched darkness. Even if the fortune weren't all that large, it would still be worth more than what he was paid for his boatload of watermelons; and the current bore it here to this spot to be found by him.

Having successfully justified his decision, the watermelon grower "was elated by visions of his careworn wife wearing the lace blouse she had so long waited for," and of his daughter playing with her new doll. With these happy visions the watermelon grower "no longer had any time for thoughts about the poor little corpse . . . the little human tragedy receded to the back of his mind where only a trace of it lingered." Here, Ussiri does not try to make any judgment about his protagonist's action. He has left it for his reader to decide.

In *On the Route of a Rabid Dog*, Ussiri displays his literary skill by subtly depicting two male characters who lose control of themselves and behave like rabid dogs. One is a lustful old man who repeatedly tries to make love to his young wife. After his efforts have proven futile, his wife

> looks into the depth of his eyes. They are staring aimessly, empty of thought, but filled with senseless pain—like the eyes of the rabid dog! She thinks of the dog that ran past her on the laterite road . . .

The other character is an alcoholic father who runs after his son trying to get his wife's money from him—"just enough for a little drink." His craving for the clear white liquor is so strong that he loses control of himself. His symptoms are exactly those of a rabid dog:

> As he chases his son for the money, saliva begins to dribble from his mouth, his swollen tongue appearing between his teeth. His breathing grows louder and he begins emitting low, animal-like cries —like the beast that has just passed out of sight.

Ussiri ends his story with the death of the rabid dog as "the sun drops behind the mountains—and dog, men and the laterite road—all dissolve into the invisible flow of time."

Like the writings of his contemporaries, some of Vanich Charungkij-anant's short stories in *Down the Same Lane,* which won the S.E.A. Write Award in 1984, are also reminiscent of the October events. But the two short stories chosen for this anthology have nothing to do with the social or political climate of the time. In both *The Song of the Leaves* and *The Barter,* Vanich seems to imply that there is no clear-cut line between the physical and spiritual world. In *The Song of the Leaves,* Vanich portrays the character of Grandma, a songstress who loves her art more than anything in the world—"to leave my husband I'm not afraid, but I won't be separated from my song . . ." For so many years she has tried to teach her granddaughter the art of singing but to no avail. Finally at the moment of Grandma's death during her last performance at the temple fair, her granddaughter comes on stage, miraculously singing Grandma's song with what is unmistakably Grandma's voice.

In *The Barter,* Vanich skillfully creates another situation in which he shows how the emotional and spiritual ties between different parts of a century-old pavilion can be so strong that any misplacement or separation can cause strange and bizarre happenings. "They have stood together for a hundred years, how can you have the heart to go and separate them." Only In *Chang,* the builder from the north who has been with this northern style pavilion all his life, knows the answer.

Short stories and poems written by S.E.A. Write awardees in the last decade show less influence of the political upheavals in the 1970s. Although some of them are equally concerned about the plight of the poor and the underprivileged, the battle cry has been toned down. The themes treated are more diverse and their renderings more experimental.

In her collection of short stories, *Jewels of Life,* Anchan displays her literary skill by using different literary techniques to convey the diversity of her themes. Unlike some contemporary writers, Anchan does not concern herself with social and political issues. She prefers to probe into different aspects of human psychology. In her story *Mother,* she paints a surrealistic picture of a mother and son relationship. The story is told through the dream-like state of mind of a son who has just lost his mother and longs for her to come back to him. In *The Beggars,* Anchan's portrayal of her two beggars, Grandpa Stump and Grandma Cross-eyed, are quite different from Khomtuan Khanthanu's beggar in *A Beggar's Chant.* Ironically, Anchan's beggars are actually the "givers". Their profession provides a path to Nirvana to a monk who blesses them. They have also been an inspiration to an artist and a writer whose works bring them both fame and fortune. And without their being conscious of it, the two beggars have made a rich, young, and beautiful singer happy because she can have someone to give money to and feel good about it. "But it's really a very good thing . . . that some awfully poor people do exist."

Phaithun Thanya, the 1987 awardee, wrote about different aspects of human behavior, using his home town, a small village in southern Thailand, as his main setting. In *People on the Bridge* he depicts two bull keepers whose stubbornness and false pride bring about their tragic deaths. In his other short story, *The Prophecy,* Phaithun sarcastically portrays the conflict between religious institution and superstitious belief by using a Buddhist temple worth a million baht and the old banyan tree as symbols. The defender of religious faith is none other than the abbot himself, while the shaman is the champion of the other camp. The conflict arises when the banyan tree has spread itself to the point that it has become a real threat to the temple. The temple or the tree—that is the question. Ironically, the conflict is solved when one of the two young men who have been hired to cut down the tree is mysteriously killed. Only the abbot seems to know who the killer is.

The latest colection of short stories to have won the S.E.A. Write Award in 1993 is by Sila Khomchai, a former activist turned social satirist. In his famous short story, *Mid-road Family,* he humorously tells of a middle-class couple who are trapped in the Bangkok traffic long enough for them to make a "family" . . ."My wife is pregnant! Do you hear? She is pregnant! We did it on the road." Another story, *"Sawdust Brain" and the Wrapping Paper*, is also a satire on a corrupt politician who is running for a seat in Parliament.

Another social critic and satirist is poet Saksiri Meesomsueb, whose collection of poems, *Those Hands Are White*, won the award in 1992. His message is daring, his prosody unconventional. According to him, the adult world which he often associates with social and religious institutions is hypocritical, insincere, and ignorant, whereas the children's world is simple, innocent, clean, and sincere. Children's hands are white but in danger of being contaminated by the gloved black hands of the adult.

The most recent 1995 awardee is a poet, Phaiwarin Khao-ngam whose collected poems, *The Banana-Stem Horse*, tells of the plight of rural people who migrate to the capital city of Bangkok. Phaiwarin recounts how rural people feel alienated from their urban surroundings and are nostalgic of their old way of life. They are proud of their cultural heritage, but they also realize that once they have been living in the city, they will also feel alienated among their own people and earlier lifestyle. They have thus become "displaced" and "homeless", and "the banana-stem horse" is their only savior.

The last S.E.A Write awardee to be mentioned is the poet laureate and National Artist Angkarn Kalayanapong whose collection of poems, *A Poet's Pledge*, won the S.E.A. Write Award in 1986. Although in 1973 Angkarn wrote a poem entitled, *October 14, The Day of Great Sorrow*, in which he lashed out against "military tyrants", his real concern has always been beyond the mundane world. In *A Poet's Pledge*, he declares his faith in the power of poetry which he believes can "cleanse the human world of sorrows:"

> I shall even refuse Nirvana
> And suffer the circling wheel of rebirths
> To translate the multitude of wonders
> Into poems dedicated to this universe
> If men grew deaf to poetry's charms

What treasures could replace the loss?
Even ashes and dust would abhor
The dryness of the wretched human soul

The short stories and poems selected for this collection should give international readers a general introduction to contemporary Thai literary works in the last two decades. However, it should be noted that all the short stories and poems represented in this anthology were originally written in Thai. In rendering these literary works into English, the translators have tried to adhere to the Thai texts and have sought to preserve the Thai flavor of the original. Admittedly, this task is not easy, especially with poetry. Nevertheless, it is hoped that the translators have managed to capture the spirit and transmit the essential message of the original works to readers whose mother tongue is not Thai.

Nitaya Masavisut

PRONUNCIATION GUIDE

The Thai words in this volume are romanized according to the Royal Institute system, except in the case of personal names, which are spelled according to personal preference. A few of the Thai Buddhist terms are romanized using the generally accepted spellings, as are some names of historical people and places.

Below is an approximate pronunciation guide. In several cases, a single English spelling is used to represent more than one sound.

CONSONANTS

Initial position:

K	SKIN
KH	KIN
P	SPIN
PH	PIN
T	STILL
TH	TILL
CH	JAR; or CHIN
NG	SING
R	trilled "r" sound

All other consonants are pronounced as in English.

VOWELS

A   ACROSS, FATHER
E   HEN, DAY
I   BIT, BEE
O   HOPE, SNOW; or SAUCE, SONG
U   BOOK, SHOE; or this "u" sound said with a wide smile

AE   HAT
OE   FUR (without "r" sound)
IA   INDIA
UA   JOSHUA; or OE + A (as in FUR and ACROSS)
AI   ICE
AO   OUT
UI   COOING
OI   COIN
IU   FEW
EO   LAY OVER
OEI   OE + I (as in FUR and BEE)
UAI   UA + I (as in JOSHUA and BEE)
AEO   AE + O (as in HAT and HOPE)
IEO   IA + O (as in INDIA and HOPE,
        similar to CLEOPATRA)

NIGHTFALL ON THE WATERWAY

USSIRI THAMMACHOT

Translated by Chamnongsri L. Rutnin

U NHURRIEDLY, the man paddled his empty boat homeward against the current. The evening sun had sunk behind the uneven outline of treetops above the banks of the *khlong*,[1] but its portent of night seemed lost on the paddler, for he continued to keep his boat moving with the same slow, tired strokes. His spirit was leaden and inert even though he felt a dull longing to be home before nightfall.

The man had been downhearted from the moment he pushed away from the market pier. His full boatload of heavy, green watermelons had brought him a sum so pitiful that he couldn't bring himself to buy the cheap lace blouse that his wife had asked him to bring her from the market—not the blouse, not even a small toy for his little daughter. Already he could hear himself telling his waiting wife, "Wait till next time . . . we didn't get enough this time." Sad and disheartened she would be, as always, and he would have to allay her sense of disappointment as best he could, perhaps telling her, "Let's save some for a rainy day."

First published in *Thai P.E.N. Anthology of Short Stories and Poems of Social Consciousness*, September 1983
1. canal

1

He had made countless trips to the market pier to sell his watermelons to the wholesale buyer, and each time he had been left with a sense of futility, a sense of wasted labor. His toil—and his wife's—had seemed as worthless as the sweat that evaporated at the touch of a sultry breeze or dripped and dissolved into the ever-moving current of the *khlong*, leaving only its moist and sticky residue that oppressed rather than vitalized. But that was the way things were—the one buyer monopolized the watermelon market. As soon as the man's boat moved alongside the pier, other melon growers whisper to him in a kinship of defeat, "Better to sell at his price than let them rot."

"We'll just have to grow more, maybe two or three times more. Then you can have something new to wear to the temple and the little one can have dolls like other children." That was what he would have to tell his waiting wife. He couldn't see any other way of earning enough to buy all the simple things that they dreamed of enjoying. Of course, it meant more back-breaking drudgery, more stoic patience, and, above all, more waiting. But then the woman was no stranger to waiting; it had become part of her life. She was always waiting for things she wanted—a cheap transistor radio to bring music into her drab life, a thin gold chain she could show off to her neighbours. These were the kinds of gifts he had promised before she came to live with him.

Just above the horizon of the darkening paddy fields, homing birds flew in flocks across a sky gloriously bathed in the gold and orange rays of the sunken sun. The trees on both banks darkened and grew patches of deep shadows that spread with a gradual ominousness. Ahead, just where the *khlong* widened and curved, thin curls of white smoke twisted softly upward from behind a dark clump of trees and disappeared into the fast paling sky. As the man paddled on in the stillness of the evening, a motorboat approached from the opposite direction, passed him, and was gone in a rush of roaring speed, churning the quiet water into a commotion of foaming trails and ruffled waves.

As he guided his lurching boat to the bank for shelter, the rushing afterwash of the motorboat rammed against its bow a mass of floating refuse and the light craft tossed and rocked precariously. The man held his paddle still and stared hard at the offending mass of flotsam; caught in it was a rubber doll bobbing to the rhythm of the disturbed water.

The man used the paddle to push away the floating garbage and picked the sodden doll out of the water for a closer look. The little toy was there in its entirety, not a part of it was missing—a naked female baby doll with red smiling lips, pale rubber skin, and big, black-painted staring pupils that somehow suggested cold eternity. He moved its limbs back and forth with great satisfaction. This little doll was going to be a companion to his lonely little girl, who would no longer be ashamed of not having a doll to play with like other kids in their neighborhood. He cheerfully imagined the joy of her bright-eyed excitement and was suddenly impatient to be home with this precious gift for her.

The brand new doll came with the current. Who its owner was was beyond his interest and speculation. The *khlong* had made its meandering way through so many villages, fields, and towns before it had reached this point. Who knew how many eyes and hands it had evaded as it drifted with this collection of refuse past countless other paddle boats and wooden piers that led down from waterside houses. He couldn't help imagining its little owner crying over her beloved doll as she watched the water carrying it irretrievably away. He could see the pathetic childish helplessness that he had seen in his own little daughter when she once dropped a juicy piece of watermelon on the dust-covered ground, and he felt a flutter of pity for the unknown child.

With a heightened sense of urgency he skillfully maneuvered his way, avoiding the vines and branches that trailed into the water. Motorboats that monopolized the center path of the waterway sent waves of agitated water towards the dark banks on either side. Occasionally he had to stop paddling and hold the paddle against the unsettled water to steady the boat, but it caused him no anger or resentment. Home was not so far away now, and the rising moon would soon be high enough for him to make his way more easily.

3

He continued to keep his boat close to the shelter of the bank, even when its overhanging vegetation had been swallowed by the velvet blackness of night. Now and then his movements startled nocturnal birds from their *khlong*-side thickets. With harsh piercing shrieks they rose in agitated flight, flapping their wings over his head, and disappeared into the darkness of the opposite bank. Their stirring scattered airborne congregations of fireflies, which flashed like intermittent sparks from a kindled fire, before settling behind dark clumps of *khlong*-side reeds like a soft luminous shower. Whenever he drifted too close to the bank, the drones of the myriad of waterside insects sounded like plaintive wails of human miseries, and an aching loneliness would sweep over him.

In a timeless moment of solitude on the lightless *khlong* with no passing boat to keep him company—a timeless moment in which the moving water made soft sounds like the breath of a dying man—he thought of death and suddenly realized that the quiet *khlong* breeze brought with it the smell of putrefaction.

A rotting carcass of some animal, he thought. A dead puppy—or perhaps a piglet—that *khlong*-side inhabitants would never hesitate to throw into the waterway, relying on the current to bear it away while nature completed the process of decay, and water finalized the disintegration of the once-living flesh. There . . . there it was . . . the source of this nauseating smell held by that mass of floating garbage under the shadow of an overspreading banyan tree.

A momentary glance, and he was about to navigate his boat away from the stinking repulsive thing when something about it caught his attention. His unbelieving eyes were drawn back to it—a rotting human corpse floating there with that mass of lifeless garbage. He was frozen with shock and fear, his paddle held in midstroke.

It took him more than a few moments to gather his courage and with his paddle push aside part of the floating garbage so that the pathetic nauseating object could move closer. With the help of the pale moonlight that glimmered coldly through the banyan leaves, he scrutinized the lifeless body with morbid curiosity.

Like the doll that he had just picked out of the water, it was a nude baby girl about the same age as his daughter. Not a part of the pitiful little dead thing was missing—yes, like the doll—except for the absence of the doll's fixed smile and black vacant stare. The child's body was horribly bloated and, in the palor of the fugitive moonbeam, had taken on a nauseating tinge of green. It was hard to imagine what this little girl had been like in the freshness of life, what bright innocence must have been hers before she became this festering corpse in the course of the sad, inevitable process that would finally make her one with the ever-moving current of this *khlong*.

The man was sharply conscious of the poignancy of the sadness and loneliness of man's individual destiny. He thought of the child's parents, of their reaction to this cruel turn of fate. What could he do to let them know? He started to turn his boat this way and that to call for help, covering his nose with the palm of his hand to block out the sickening stench of the corpse that became unbearable each time a breeze wafted from its direction.

Turning away to look for a passing boat, he involuntarily glanced back and caught sight of a glint that made his eyes widen. Almost entirely buried in the bloated flesh of the dead child's wrist was a slim chain of yellow metal. The sight of it in the moonlight inflated his heart and made it miss a beat.

"Gold!" he cried inwardly, stretching out his paddle to move the pathetic swollen little body closer. The sudden roar of a motorboat and the light from its kerosene lamp made him jump with guilt. He turned his boat so that its shadow fell on the corpse, hiding it from view, and waited until he was alone again in the silence that followed. It would have been a gross injustice, an unforgivable stupidity, to let someone else take the prize away from him. He would not let anyone take advantage of him now as they did when he sold his watermelons. After all, he was the discoverer of this treasure, he had suffered the dreadful company of this bloated corpse, he had borne its unbearable stench in this moon-blanched darkness. Even if the fortune weren't that much, it would still be worth more than what he was paid for his boatload of water-melons; and, after all, the current had born it here to this spot to be found by him.

He was elated by visions of his careworn wife wearing the lace blouse she had so long waited for; perhaps he would even buy her one of those prettily colored *phanung*[2] from the north to go with it, and he would get clothes for their child and for himself. For the first time he would enjoy the happiness of spending without the twinges of pain that always came from the parting with hard-earned money. What did he have to do to earn it but paddle home against the current which he had to do anyway? The happiness that would light up the drained face of his wife and the eagerness that would shine in his child's eyes, short-lived and transient though they might be, were blessings as precious to his joyless life as a shower to a drought-parched paddy field.

The moonlight lay a rippled silver sheen on the moving water, and the seemingly interminable hum of insects now resembled prayers chanted for the dead. He held his breath and, with the thin blade of his melon knife, cut into the soft swollen flesh of the fingers and hand of the dead child. Piece by piece the decomposing flesh fell away from the white bones and was carried away by the drifting current, gradually exposing the bright chain of gold that it had almost hidden from view with its ghastly swelling. The stench was so strong that he gagged for air, and by the time he had the prize in his hand, he could no longer refrain from retching. The horrible smell of death clung to his knife, his hand, and his entire body. Vomiting copiously into the water, he washed his knife and hands, letting the water carry away every disgusting trace of what he had done, just as it had carried away the pieces of the dead child's flesh.

The corpse, freed with a push from the paddle, was drifting slowly downstream, further and further away, in silent finality. The man pushed his boat away from the bank, guiding it to midstream. The doll lying face up in the middle of the boat caught his eyes. It

2. Thai sarong

was lying there with the fixed smile on its red lips and the blank stare in its painted black eyes, its hands stuck up in the empty air as if begging for pity. "It's haunted! It's that little girl's," he thought, and hurriedly pitched the doll into the water so that it drifted away in the same direction as its owner. "So what!" he thought, his heart filled with elation. He could buy another one, or even two such dolls, for his daughter to play with and amuse herself. He was no longer depressed with what he had thought was a futile trip. Thinking of his wife and child who were as yet ignorant of their unexpected luck, he paddled as fast as he could with a new-found energy until the lights from his home came in sight from behind the bushes not so far ahead.

He no longer had any time for thoughts about the poor little corpse. He no longer cared where it came from or whether the parents would learn of their child's fate. The little human tragedy receded to the back of his mind where only a trace of it lingered.

The man quickened the strokes of his paddle with unaccustomed vigor and exuberance.

ON THE ROUTE OF
A RABID DOG

USSIRI THAMMACHOT

Translated by Chamnongsri L. Rutnin

T HE fiery heat of the sun bakes the small laterite road
that leads to the village. The roadside shrubs droop in the
heat, their leaves so weighed down by the dry red dust that
they hang motionless in the wind. The sun rides high in the bright
empty sky. Its hard, hot rays stream down onto the rough laterite
road that is deserted by animals and wayfarers this midsummer
afternoon.

In the distance where the road winds down the small rise in the
dry ground, a small black speck comes jigging into view. As it
moves, it takes the shape of a four-legged animal heading straight
towards the village . . .

It is a dark brown dog, terribly thin, covered with dry red dust.
Something invisible needles it into a constant state of fear, for it
runs at an even pace, neither fast nor slow, never seeming to tire.

Its eyes are wide open—empty and staring, like the eyes of a
sinful, aimless, unhappy human being.

In a house by the side of that road, a rough and simple house
like those of all the villagers, a thin old man glares furiously at his
young wife. The hair on his head is wispy and sparse, its black
strands outnumbered by silvery grey ones. It sticks up haphazardly,
catching the meager sunlight that shines through the slits in the

bamboo walls. His pathetic skeletal-like body is bare above the checkered sarong that he usually wears when in the house.

Is she in love with another man? Suspicion grows as he looks at his young wife half reclining on the bed. Though she has borne him two children, he cannot surpress his jealous urges. After all, not a man in the village would refuse the lushness of a body like hers if she offered it. Maybe she has. Lately she has always been reluctant when he wants to make love to her.

"What's the matter? The children aren't home," he tries to suppress the tremble in his voice.

"I'm bored with it. You take so long each time," she makes a move to open the shutters.

"What d'you expect. I'm not a young man. Don't you open those shutters!" he says menacingly.

"Then act like an old man!" she throws back at him. "Why do it in the daytime. It's darned hot!"

"Eh, eh!" he cries. "It hasn't always been like this. Who have you been playing around with? Who's been f . . . ing you that's made you so bored with me? I'll kill you if I catch you at it!" He jabs his finger at her face, literally jumping around in jealous fury.

"You've gone mad! Sex has made you mad," she shouts and then steadies herself as he charges at her.

A sharp push at his bony chest makes him stagger back. And as she rises to her feet, he strikes her on the mouth with the veined and boney back of his hand. The blow is strong enough to make her fall back into her former position.

She touches her bleeding lips with her slim hand, looking up at his glittering eyes as he looms over her.

"This is what you're good at, isn't it." she sneers, her full breast heaving under the *phanung* [1] that is wrapped around it. As she looks at his awkward, corpse-like body, she thinks of the day, long ago, when she eloped with him, leaving her father's home, to live with him here in this house by the laterite road.

---

1. Thai sarong, in this case worn up to the armpits in the style for bathing

9

He was handsome, and as strong as an elephant. His love making was forceful, and yet gentle: as soft as the wind and as unyielding as a rock. All those qualities have been sapped by time. His journey has been longer than hers—much longer. Sexuality in him has grown sick and decrepit. It is no longer under his control.

He has changed into another man—pathetically filled with lust and jealousy.

To her, this state of things is agonizing and unbearable.

"You are going mad," she says out of bitterness rather than intention.

"Yes, mad. You unfaithful bitch!" he screeches, his clawlike hands grasping towards her throat.

She throws herself at him with an unexpected force that throws him against the bamboo wall of the hut. She hears him swearing and cursing as she races out of the door. The young woman runs towards the laterite road, one hand holding the knot of the *phanung* above her breast, the other pulling its hem above her knees. Looking back, she sees he is right on her heels.

As she is just about to cross the road to the paddy field on the other side, she hears his frantic call,

"Rabid dog! Stop, stop! Don't cross the road. That dog has rabies."

She stops and feels her knees turning to jelly so that she has to sit down in the dust beside the road. The deathly thin dog, covered with red dust, passes in front of her.

It turns its empty eyes on her, snarls, and runs straight ahead on the empty road, never changing its pace. It runs on steadily at the same unchanging pace. Its tail hangs stiffly between its hind legs.

She remains sitting in a heap on the ground, sobbing with fear and anger.

"The dog has rabies." He is standing behind her. "Lucky it didn't bite you."

Still breathing hard, he bends down to touch her bare shoulder and says in a slow, lingering tone, "If it had bitten you, you would have died like *Ai* Phan last year. Remember how he wailed and howled like a dog before he died? Come on, let's go home. I'm not angry any more."

On the bed in the dim light of the tightly shuttered house, the elderly man toils over his wife's body. He tries again and again to retrieve the virility of his youthful years, to have it at his beck and call as it once used to be. It seems to him like trying to climb a steep hill with aching legs that oppose his will at every step. Something in him has become either treacherous or crippled beyond recall.

The young woman lets her old husband move on her body without much expectation. She knows that efforts are futile without some great miracle. With the light that seeps into the house, she can see the sweat bathe his wrinkled face. Their breathing, his and hers, sounds loud against the breath of the wind outside.

She looks into the depth of his eyes. They are staring aimlessly, empty of thought, but filled with senseless pain—like the eyes of the rabid dog! She thinks of the dog that ran past her on the laterite road . . .

The thin, dust-covered dog runs straight ahead on the road leading into the village. The sun has moved in the direction of the tall mountain range. Its heat has eased somewhat. The dog runs past the grass and shrubs whose leaves are weighed down by the heavy red dust from the laterite. It is running at a slower pace and a stiffer gait than before. It goes on running past roadside houses and barns that look benumbed by the dense heat of the summer afternoon.

It lets out low painful cries. Its breathing is hard and loud. Sticky saliva trails from its stiff jaws . . .

The small boy watches his father searching the shelf with quick nervous movements for some time before asking,

"What are you looking for?"

His father turns sharply.

"Mother's money? There isn't any," the boy says.

"How d'you know? Has she taken it all?" the father asks, going on with his nervous search.

The boy smiles, starting to enjoy the situation.

"No, she put it somewhere else. She said if she kept it on the shelf, you'd take it all to buy drink."

"Ha, you know!" the father bends down to smile sweetly at his son. "Come on, tell me where she has put it."

The boy looks up at the father whose breath stinks of alcohol and shakes his head in answer to the pleading in the man's eyes.

"Come on, when your mother comes back she'll give it to me anyway. Tell me where it is."

"Nope."

"You're stubborn, just like your mother," the father turns to look around nervously, not knowing where to continue his search.

An old photograph on the wall catches his eye.

The photograph is in a faded yellow frame. It has meant nothing to him for such a very long time. Now he studies it—a full length studio portrait of himself and his wife standing in front of a painted background, a make-believe scene of a bright blue sea, with a boat whose sail hides part of the grey mountains. Painted palms with beautiful, curved trunks are laden with coconuts.

Looking at the photograph, he laughs to himself—the newly wedded couple and their dream! That painted cardboard sea with the mountains, boat and coconut palm represented their dream. They had dreams of seeing a white beach and the wide sea once in their lives, of breathing the air from the boundless river that stretched out until it touched the sky, of watching the beautiful people who laughed and played there.

For a brief moment laughter stirs in his withered heart. How crazy we were! Now we know that we shall never see the sea, not in our next ten lives!

Wave upon wave of nausea rises in his throat. He walks towards the framed photograph, but the watchful boy is quicker. The child leaps forward and draws a white envelope from the back of the frame.

"Heh, let me see how much there is," cries the thwarted father. "What business is it of yours?"

"Mother told me to take care of it."

"I won't take it all. Just enough for a little drink—I'm going to give it up soon."

"Nope," the boy sidles towards the door.

"You'll get hurt if you don't give it to me," he scolds, trying to bar the door with his arm. His thoughts are full of the taste of liquor that is to come in the late afternoon drinking bout.

The boy darts out of the door, his father pursuing closely at his heels.

At that point of the laterite road, the village is very close by. The child bounds across the road right in front of the thin, dust covered dog that is heading towards the village. The boy pays no attention to its snarl. He continues to run without hearing his father's frantic call,

"Hey, stop. A rabid dog!"

The little boy does not look back.

The father lets out his breath in relief when his son manages to safely cross the path of the rabid animal. In his mind he can see the agonizing death of Phan, his neighbor. With his own eyes, he has seen Phan die from the bite of a rabid dog. The thought makes his skin crawl with fear and disgust. Rabid dogs! They are horrible, dangerous beasts that everyone should avoid.

There it goes, breathing noisily, emitting low cries. Sticky saliva dribbles from its stiff jaws . . .

Waves of nausea are rising again, one after another. It comes on suddenly. The longing for the clear, white liquid drives all other thoughts out of his head. The boy is already far down the paddy fields. He races after him, cursing with anger.

Running over rough, parched ground, together with his chronic alcoholism and a craving for the clear white liquor, causes him to stiffen his jaws.

As he chases his son for the money, saliva begins to dribble from his mouth, his swollen tongue appearing between his teeth. His breathing grows louder and he begins emitting low, animal-like cries—like the beast that has just passed out of sight . . .

The sun moves lower and is partially hidden by the mountain range. Its bright, copper rays suffuse the western sky. The laterite road that runs across the village looks dark against the glow of the sunset.

At this evening hour, the thin brown dog covered with dry red dust runs along the laterite road into the village . . .

. . . And falls down, dead.

Red dust sticks to the saliva around its mouth, its body stiff, its eyes open and its swollen tongue jammed between its jaws.

THE sun drops behind the mountains. The copper redness at the hem of the sky dims. All visible things become deep shadows in the dimness. Dogs, men and the laterite road—all dissolve into the invisible flow of time.

THE SONG OF THE LEAVES

VANICH CHARUNGKIJ-ANANT

Translated by Chamnongsri L. Rutnin

G RANDMA rinsed her bowl after having used it to pour water into the ground as an act of merit-sharing with sundry acquaintances and relatives who had passed away. *I* [1] Somchao, her eighteen-year-old granddaughter, wandered by to steal a look at Grandma—probably fearing the old woman might black out and drown. The girl had often told the old woman that the bowl could easily be washed in the house—that there wasn't any need to come down to the pier to wash it. But Grandma would say that the pier was so close, there was no reason to waste the water in the jar—especially now that the river had risen so high that she didn't even have to go down the steps, making things so easy.

Grandma didn't in the least fear what vexed her granddaughter. She wasn't afraid of fainting and drowning, not even when the river was so swollen and the current so swift. So familiar with this river, she was—born from it.

In Grandma's young days, the pier wasn't where it was now. She remembered having to walk from the house down to the pier. There used to be a sprawling guava tree and a richly foliaged

1. title used before a woman's first name or nickname, traditionally derogatory but also used with close relatives and friends

banyan tree growing out there. Now they were all gone—Grandma couldn't remember when. Long ago, it was.

The swift current carried off a bit of the bank each year, especially in the eleventh and twelfth months when the water gushed straight into the bank where Grandma's house stood. The land on the opposite side grew and grew. The Suphan River was more winding now than in Grandma's girlhood days.

The house that in those days had stood a good way from the river now had the front stilts, which held up the wooden verandah, in the water. One day the house would collapse, Grandma thought.

Grandma worried. Where would *I* Somchao go if the house fell?

Grandma walked up from the pier not forgetting to fill the bowl with water for the jasmine that grew beside the wooden steps. The plant had always provided Grandma with white flowers for stringing into "raggedy garlands" for the Buddha image. "Raggedy garlands" was *I* Somchao's cynical way of saying that Grandma's handiwork didn't look anything like garlands.

"So what! I'm only a village woman, not a palace lady!"

That was what she told *I* Somchao, and went on stringing garlands in her own style, sharpening one end of the wooden part of a joss stick while cutting a nick in the other end for tying the string. *I* Somchao told her to use a needle but Grandma said that her poor old eyes couldn't see well enough to thread a needle.

But when Somchao offered to thread the needle for her, Grandma refused and scolded her for not minding her own business.

Grandma wanted *I* Somchao to learn her songs but Somchao wouldn't do it no matter how much Grandma urged her. She said Grandma's songs were so crude that she would never dare to sing them. Grandma retorted that it wasn't that she didn't *dare*, she just *couldn't*. Grandma had tried to teach her the art of the songs for so many years before finally giving up.

The old woman used to begin the song for Somchao to join in. Grandma opened the song with, "Oei [2] . . . , the old *kaew* tree,

2. sound signaling the opening of traditional folk songs

16

your branches're heavy with blossoms so white . . ." and stopped, waiting to see when *I* Somchao would come out with the next line, but the girl would only laugh or simply remain silent. Then, after a while, she would get irritable and say that she would not learn the songs, she didn't like them, and she couldn't sing. The girl actually prefered *luk thung*[3] songs but she couldn't sing them either. No, *I* Somchao had never sung any real song, just hummed or made simple little tunes. In fact, she never spoke very much at all. Some people even called her "dumb Somchao".

Grandma had to continue herself. "Oei . . . , the old *kaew* tree, your branches're heavy with blossoms so white, close by and upright stands the tall *krang* tree, scattering its berries all over the ground . . ."

It had been over seventy years, but Grandma remembered these lines very clearly. She was only twelve or thirteen in those days when she used to sneak off from her father's house to learn the art of the songs from *Pho* Phet[4] at the house with the big fence behind Wat Lao Thong. *Pho* Phet would open the song with these very lines: "Oei . . . , the old *kaew* tree, your branches're heavy with blossoms so white . . ." and no one else could think up the next lines except Grandma. In *Pho* Phet's yard grew a *kaew* bush full of white blossoms. A big *krang* tree towered nearby, the ground underneath it was covered with hundreds of its small round berries. That's why Grandma came out with the lines "close by and upright stands the tall *krang* tree, scattering its berries all over the ground . . ."

Grandma stepped out on the frail wooden verandah that looked down on the river to lay down the large spoon that she used to ladle the rice into the alms bowls of the monks. Beside it, she placed the bowl in which she took the rice to give as alms to the monks each morning, turning the bowl upside down to dry. The weather-worn old wooden flooring shook and swayed when Grandma walked out to collect two brightly colored sarongs that she had hung out to dry overnight. Feeling them still damp, she

3. popular modern folk music
4. Songster Phet

17

left them where they were. Tonight was the night of the *kathin*[5] festival at Wat Pa or "the forest temple". A month ago *Mae Khwanchit*[6] had told Grandma about it and said that the organizers had wanted to have the *i-saew*[7] songs. That was why Grandma brought out the two bright sarongs which hadn't been worn for so long. She had sniffed at them and, finding them to be musty, had washed them.

Grandma had told Somchao yesterday to be ready for the temple fair tonight. The girl said that she couldn't have forgotten even if she had wanted to because Grandma had told her the same thing over and over about ten times. Grandma wanted Somchao to go with her because she could at least sing the refrain along with the others. Grandma had given up hoping that she would ever become the second or the third in the line of songstresses. If she didn't want to try then there was nothing Grandma could do.

These days Suphan Buri River was quiet and serene. Only a few boats passed by each day, unlike last year when motor boats and long-tailed boats created an almost constant ear-splitting din. Since the asphalt roads were built, leading to just about everywhere, nobody wanted to use the motor boats and the long-tailed boats. Only the traders' barges, with their strings of boats and other barges in tow, made their way along the river at infrequent intervals.

In the days when Grandma was a young girl, the river was as serene as it was today. Paddle boats were the only traffic. But once in a long while boisterous sounds shattered the tranquility, and those were the times of temple fairs and traditional merit-making. It was on those occasions when she had followed the singers to the festivals at Wat Pa that she really became able to absorb the intricacies of the song. In those times, the people of her village would paddle their boats to the main town of the province. Grandma as a little girl would go along with them. They would paddle along in a jolly procession of twenty or thirty boats, singing

5. annual festival at which new robes are presented to monks

6. Songstress Khwanchit

7. one kind of traditional folk entertainment

songs that reverberated along the banks of the river.

In front of the riverside mansion of Chao Phraya Yomarat, songsters used to float their paddle boats close together like an enormous raft and sing *phleng rua* or boat songs for the nobleman of the mansion. The singers of Grandma's village often came home with the prize money.

Grandma herself had personally won a fine reward when she was still young but already well versed in the art. She could still recall that there had been a boat of men from the neighboring province of Ang Thong that had stopped to challenge her boat of women. What the *pho phleng* or the songster's name was she couldn't remember. What she could recall was the extreme darkness of his skin because Grandma had retorted to his challenge with, "Oei . . . , Hearing a voice ever so bright and clear, I had to peer out to take a good glance, oh where's that singing man from Ang Thong, first sight of him almost sent me into the water, oh dear sir so very black are you, is it true that you live at the 'Golden Bowl'? And do you burn charcoal or do you grow rice?"

Chao Phraya Yomarat so enjoyed this repartee that he actually gave Grandma the generous reward of five baht.

Grandma had "played the songs" all her life, travelling up and down the country on countless waterways. Ang Thong, Singburi, Uthai Thani, Ayutthaya—she had been through all those provinces. When it came to the game of songs, Grandma wasn't afraid of anyone. Whether it was *phleng rua, phleng choi,* or *i-saew,* or any of their special variations, she could sing them all.

Grandma went into the kitchen, spooned some rice onto a plate and sat down to eat it using her fingers. She ate the rice with *nam phrik*, the shrimp paste chili dip she had made the day before. With it there was fresh morning glory and the subtle flavored yellow *sano* flower, both lightly scalded, and the salted fish made by Somchao. Having finished the meal, Grandma washed the plates, filled a pail with water and took a rag from the top of the steps, damping it to clean the floor.

Grandma cleaned the floor by wiping it with the damp rag everyday, morning and evening. She just squatted down and did it bit by bit—it didn't take all that long. Somchao had tried to stop her from doing this chore, to no avail. The girl finally stopped trying, saying that the old woman was like a stubborn child.

"I can do it, can't I? This house is only as big as the space it takes a cat to have its dying throes!" Grandma used the time-worn simile to support her point.

This little house was very old indeed. Built by Grandma's long-dead parents, it now leaned precariously to one side due to age and the creeping erosion of the river bank.

It was where Grandma was born. Her three siblings were now all dead. Grandma had a husband when she was eighteen. It happened that a young fellow from Ban Makham Lom, a nearby village, saw her when she went to Suan Hong Temple to "sing the songs". With the help of his gang of friends he had abducted her. They had a daughter—*I* Somchao's mother. But Grandma had stayed with her husband for only two years because he kept insisting that she give up the songs.

Her love for the songs was deep and boundless . . . "even when in the hands of the demon, I went on longing for you, to leave my husband I'm not afraid, I won't be separated from my songs . . ."

Grandma still remembered the song she improvised when singing with her songster friends soon after she regained her single status. Her husband came several times to plead with her to come back to live with him, but Grandma was adamant. No matter what, she would go on with her life of songs. Eventually, the husband took their daughter to his village to take care of her.

I Somchao's mother came to live here with Grandma after her own husband died. She soon died, too, leaving *I* Somchao with Grandma . . . The problem was that she went and took a husband when she was too old, so she died before her child was big enough to be of any use to her—that was what Grandma used to tell her friends.

Somchao was about five or six when her mother died. The orphan was raised by Grandma who earned a living from her songs. When no one hired her to sing, she picked the guava and the *maprang* and sold them to earn the money to feed *I* Somchao.

Grandma often felt worried about *I* Somchao—how would the

girl live when Grandma was no longer here! No matter how much Grandma told her to learn the songs, she wouldn't even make a start. If Somchao knew the songs, she would at least have some work to keep her body and soul together. It didn't matter if she became only a second rate songster, because Grandma could ask *Mae* Khwanchit to make some use of her. As it was, the girl could only sing the refrain—what good would she be to anyone?

After cleaning the floor with the rag, Grandma lay down to sleep. Nowadays, Grandma's days were almost equally divided between waking and sleeping. Grandma never went far out of the village except on her singing missions. She had some small savings which she asked Somchao to keep for her funeral. Most of the savings came from her singing but last year the amount had diminished mainly became the four or five *maprang* trees bore almost no fruit.

In the days when all the master songsters and mistress songstresses of her generation were still alive, Grandma earned quite a lot of money. At that time, Grandma didn't think she would remain alive this long, and she didn't know that there was going to be *I* Somchao to look after. So she spent most of the money she earned in making religious merit like giving alms. Now Grandma had to be very frugal indeed, even refraining from buying a new *phanung* to wear.

Most of the songsters and songstresses of her generation had died—*Mae* Tuan, *Pho* Phrom, *I* Chua, *Nai* Tom and *Mae* Ning. Only *I* Thonglo was still alive. The woman talked far too much but Grandma still wanted to see her again. The only times they met were for the songs. *I* Thonglo must be terribly old by now, like Grandma herself.

When Grandma was asleep, Somchao would wander off to some of the neighbors' houses to borrow those filmstar magazines with pictures and stories of the stars. Whenever Grandma went anywhere to sing, Somchao would always accompany her—at least she could be put to use in singing the refrains or marking the rhythm with the wooden clappers or the metal *ching* [8] or merely

8. Thai cymbals

21

by clapping her hands. Somchao deigned to go just because Grandma went; if Grandma couldn't go Somchao wouldn't go either.

There was once, the one and only occasion, that Grandma couldn't make it—and that was when she hadn't the strength to stand up. Even though she couldn't stand up, Grandma had insisted that she was going. Somchao, however, wouldn't let her go and went out to ask the people who came to invite Grandma whether they really wanted Grandma to die.

Somchao rarely opened her mouth to speak. She had absolutely no interest in the songs. She didn't care how many people praised Grandma as a top-class songstress. The girl liked *luk thung* songs and had dreamt that she might go and dance in the *luk thung* chorus. But of course it was just a day dream she wasn't even attractive, and then there was Grandma to be looked after—she rejected the possibility of actually realizing her fantasy.

Somchao completed grade four at Wat Manao temple school. She didn't pursue her studies any further, nor did she look for work anywhere. People had asked her if she would like to go with them to work in the factories. Somchao would have liked to go because the *luk thung* song about Chantana, the factory girl, was a great hit. Grandma wouldn't have stopped her from going, but somehow Somchao changed her mind and didn't go. Maybe it was because some people asked if she really had the heart to leave Grandma who was so old.

But Grandma had been the one to tell Somchao, "You go where you want to. Don't you worry about me." That was because Grandma was already resigned to the fact that Somchao would never take up singing the songs.

Somchao's routine work was looking after the fruit trees and planting a vegetable garden. Not that there were that many trees, Grandma's land being such a small piece. It used to be much bigger but the river had taken it bit by bit each passing year. Growing in the garden were the four or five *maprang* trees, one *thong dam* mango tree, the guava and some *lamut* trees. When the sapodilla season came around, Grandma and Somchao would pick the fruit, take it to the market in the provincial town and bring back the modest proceeds to buy the necessities of life.

The only other income source was the songs, but it was now no longer a reliable one. Some years ago, the great *Mae* Khwanchit had come to ask Grandma to go and sing with her troupe. That day, Grandma's old eyes had filled with tears of pride. And because Somchao had gone along with Grandma, *Mae* Khwanchit actually taught her to mark the beats and sing the refrains.

Before Somchao's mother had died, Grandma went to live in Bangkok, somewhere in the Nonthaburi area. She stayed with a distant relative and took care of his children. The reason she went was to be near her songster and songstress friends, they could then come together conveniently whenever they were needed at fairs or shows. At that time there were enough occasions for the songs. Grandma was happy to earn money for use in making merit.

When *Mae* Tuan died, followed by *Pho* Phrom, Grandma began to feel lonely. The friends who used to "sing the songs" with her died off one by one. Some died before *Mae* Tuan and *Pho* Phrom, some after, until almost no one was left. Grandma forced herself to remain at Nonthaburi until the death of Somchao's mother brought her back to Suphan Buri.

Back at Suphan Buri, Grandma took care of *I* Somchao. She had no other close relatives living anywhere else. Even here the relatives of her own generation were all dead and gone, leaving only the younger generations with whom she had no close ties. Grandma wasn't rich, no one wanted to bother her and she had no desire to bother anyone.

Grandma had managed to live on her income from the fruit and the songs. Once in a while, a long while, she went to Bangkok when someone asked her to sing the songs with them. She had even gone on television. Lately, though, she would go whenever *Mae* Khwanchit wanted her, and sometimes *Pho* Wai would come and invite her, too. Though Grandma was this old, her wits were still sharp and her retorts in the songs were second to none—fearless and resourceful they were. Besides, her voice was still clear and resonant. It had always been so, ever since she was a young girl.

Grandma woke up in the afternoon. She put the betel leaf and areca nut in her mouth and chewed for a little while before discarding the fibre. She felt that they didn't taste good. Grandma was never particular about her betel and areca. She had always enjoyed it no matter whether the areca was unripe or dried, whether the betel leaf was fresh or pressed. But today she didn't enjoy the taste of them in the least. She tried another mouthful and stood up only to flop down on the floor.

Grandma spat out the betel and areca. She felt unwell. She could tell that she was very ill because it was the first time ever that she had failed to enjoy her betel and areca. The old woman felt neither excitement nor fear, for she and death had been close companions for a long time. At her age, most of her friends were long dead. Grandma was familiar with death, she had been preparing for it for such a long time, making plenty of merit to allow her soul passage in the right direction.

Grandma thought of her commitment tonight and gathered all her strength to sit up. A good thing that she would be travelling by car—not like the old days when she had to walk a lot of the way. In those days if they were to sing in a hilly area, they would have to walk, and sometimes it took all day. In the eleventh and twelfth months when the water was high though, they would mostly paddle their way on boats.

Grandma was annoyed with herself for being ill at this important time. She tried to stand up again but the dizziness in her head sent her staggering into the wooden wall with an impact that shook the old house. She lay down again and closed her eyes, exhausted to the point of feeling as if her heartstring would snap.

"Maybe I won't be able to sing the songs with them tonight," Grandma murmured to herself before falling into a sleep with the thought that everything would be all right because the money she had asked Somchao to keep for her would be enough for the funeral.

"Oei . . . , the old *kaew* tree, your branches're heavy with blossoms so white, close by and upright stands the tall *krang* tree, scattering its fruit on the ground, the *sakae* has put forth his branches, who was it that cut the *tako* trunk, and left the stump sticking up among the curly *ngon kai*, the *krang* leaves have grown old and dry, not catching people's eyes as they used to, when comes the blowing breeze, the old leaves get blown away . . . blown far, far away . . ."

Where did the *i-saew* song come from? It seemed to pierce Grandma's ears, startling her eyes open. She sat up to look toward the top of the house steps, but saw nobody. She looked all around the house and still could see no one. It must have been a voice within her ears, and that reminded her of tonight's work. What time was it now? She didn't know.

Grandma made a determined effort to rise again, very slowly. She didn't want *I* Somchao to see any signs of sickness and get bossy telling her grandmother not to go to sing the songs tonight.

Grandma shouted to *I* Somchao and heard her voice answering from somewhere at the back of the house. Grandma called out her orders that Somchao should get ready for the car that was coming to fetch them and take them to Wat Pa, so that they had enough time to stop on the way to pay homage to *Luang Pho* To. Had Somchao forgotten that they had to go and sing tonight? Somchao called back to ask what was the hurry, it was only one o'clock.

That made Grandma sit down and look pensively out at the river beyond the verandah. The Suphan River was flowing with a torrential swiftness, its current twisting into great spirals right where Grandma's house stood. Big clumps of water weeds came floating by at intervals, some of them turning in a circle in front of the house before continuing on their watery way. Some of the clumps were so enormous that had the current thrown them against one of the wooden stilts, the house might well have collapsed.

The "cha-ha-hai" part of the refrains sounded somewhere in Grandma's consciousness, as if coming from that distant bend in river.

"Opening my lips to bid goodbye, both my eyes are filled with tears, oh dear heart how I think of you, how I'll miss you dear brother, in the twelfth month of the swelling tide, when the water rises between the banks, though I must take my leave, I am so grieved at our parting, take care paddling home your boat, for if you chose the wrong paddle, you might fall into the river and drown . . ."

The song sounded disjointed, now clear, now lost. Grandma looked dreamily at the river, smiling to herself.

Grandma arrived at Wat Pa, all dressed and well-speckled with powder. *I* Somchao had tried to stop her from going after seeing her condition that afternoon, but Grandma had insisted "I'm all right. I can go. I want to pay my homage to *Luang Pho* To[9], too."

Once she had finished dressing and winding the breast cloth around her chest and over one shoulder, Grandma's eyes shone brightly and looked for all the world as if the illness had vanished completely. Somchao, who had kept a close watch on her grandmother felt rather relieved. But, knowing full well that Grandma always seemed fresh and full of life whenever she was about to "sing the songs", the girl didn't feel any real confidence about Grandma's condition. Grandma had shown strange symptoms when the car arrived to fetch them at the house. That was when Somchao had tried to wake her from her nap. Grandma seemed to be unconscious. Somchao had to do so much shaking and calling before Grandma could be woken.

Somchao had kept so close to Grandma that the old woman had to chase her away to get herself dressed, not forgetting to hand the girl a thin gold chain to put around her wrist. Grandma believed that Somchao, being a young girl, should wear some gold ornaments when meeting people. The old woman told the girl not to worry about her. And so, like Grandma, Somchao got dressed in the only brightly-colored clothes that she owned.

Grandma made her way to the front of the stage. The stage, Grandma felt, was her birthplace as well as the place in which she had grown into adulthood, reached maturity and passed into old age. Everything was familiar no matter where she looked. Dancing and singing songs were so easy and so much fun. Even the specks of dust on the floor were familiar. Yes, Grandma knew every granule of dust on this stage.

That was what Grandma really felt.

9. huge statue of the Buddha

"Raising this tray above my head, I pay homage to the Triple Gems, with lighted candle and sweet incense, to the four directions I raise the *bai si*,[10] in respect to the spirits of this place, to the grace of good angels, to my teacher named *Pho* Phet, who's made me mistress of songs in Suphan, it was he who taught me the *i-saew* songs . . ."

Grandma's resonant voice extolled the teachers of the songs. It mesmerized some people into an attentive silence, while those who were not interested in the songs went on chatting and boozing. Grandma hardly ever noticed how many people were listening or not listening to her songs. Right now her entire consciousness was centered on what was taking place on the stage. She listened to the master songster, what was he singing? . . . "Don't you ever leave an opening where I can get at you!"

In any case, Grandma didn't want to look towards the audience because her eyes were so blurred that she could hardly see a thing.

Grandma forced herself to stand firm and concentrated on the voices of the master songsters and mistress songstresses, waiting for her moment.

Then Grandma went out to sing a brief opening *kroen* song and sang a retort to the master's cheeky approach. When she stumbled into a fellow songstress, the audience broke into an affectionate laughter.

They thought that Grandma was clumsy from age, but they were wrong—Grandma's eyes could no longer see.

No one on the stage saw anything out of the ordinary in Grandma, not even Somchao herself, because Grandma's old face was wreathed in smiles, her voice as vibrant as ever.

"Oh you smiling man of the moon, with your jerky monkey gait, has your head ever been hit, with nice big weighty cane? You annoy me so much, uttering such silly words. How can you be trusted, when your hair's so fuzzed, and your eyes so bulged?"

Nobody noticed anything unusual in Grandma, not even when she stepped backwards into a wooden bench. She put out her hand to feel the bench in order to locate the seat and sat down on it,

10. rice wrapped in a banana leaf, an auspicious ceremonial ornament

looking as if this was something she normally did. After all, she was too old to be standing for long. That was what everybody thought.

Somchao stopped working the clappers to come to Grandma to ask if she wanted anything. Grandma smiled at her and said "I want some betel and areca."

Somchao led Grandma to the side of the stage, eased her into a chair, picked up the betel box and put it on her lap. Grandma arranged the betel and areca, keeping her bright eyes on the master songster who was coming out with strings of razor-sharp words. From the audience, laughter at the battle of the songs between the songsters and songstresses broke out intermittently.

Grandma could no longer see anything at all, but she still had strength to put the betel into her mouth.

Grandma didn't chew the betel. She didn't know whether it tasted good or not. She could no longer taste it at all.

On the stage, Somchao stumbled. She laid down the clappers and danced out ever so smartly.

It was during the *chom dong*—or the admiring of the forest— that the songs reached the part where the man was taking his new wife home.

"Oei . . . , the old *kaew* tree, your branches're heavy with blossoms so white, close by and upright stands the tall *krang* tree, scattering its berries on the ground, the *sakae* has put forth his branches, who was it that cut the *tako* trunk, and left the stump sticking up among the curley *ngoen kai*, the *krang* leaves have grown old and dry, not catching people's eyes as they used to, when comes the blowing breeze, the old leaves get blown away . . . blown far, far away . . ."

Somchao had got that far with her singing when all the songsters and songstresses as well as all the lesser singers rushed around to take hold of her while *Mae* Khwanchit, the leader of the troupe, ran towards Grandma shouting her name.

Somchao's voice was so unmistakably Grandma's.

THE BARTER

VANICH CHARUNGKIJ-ANANT

Translated by Chamnongsri L. Rutnin

S EVERAL people were involved in this story, but the man who might be labelled as "the instigator" was an architect, a graduate from one of those universities in the West. He hit upon the idea after having been entrusted with the project—the project of building the grandest Thai-style riverside restaurant in the Bangkok metropolis.

But then, it wouldn't be fair to put the entire blame on him because the owner, too, played a signficant role in the affair. The owner was a millionaire in his fifties who felt that too much of his money was lying idle. Consequently, he wanted to invest it in something praiseworthy—and laudable in taste.

After some discussions with his friends as to the ways and means, he decided to open a restaurant. It was to be a Thai restaurant—a waterside Thai restaurant with part of the building extending over the Chao Phraya River, that "River of Kings". He summoned the architect to listen to the concept he had in mind. It was clear that the capital investment posed no problem as long as the right site was found and things went according to his wishes.

One day, therefore, they all boarded a boat and cruised along the Chao Phraya River. It was on this occasion that they found a large mansion, staid and proud, standing on the river bank.

Somber green in color and venerable in age, its dimensions were impressive even when viewed from the river at a considerable distance. It was built in the European style which had been the vogue in the latter part of King Rama V's reign. Everyone in the boat was seized by the same thought.

The navigator headed the boat for the mansion.

Though the owner wasn't living in it, the group knew that the mansion had once belonged to a nobleman with the exalted rank of Chao Phraya, and that it had been built more than sixty years ago. Every single board was solid teak, as was every tiny wooden component of the building. For ventilation, a clerestory of ornamental openwork in European gingerbread style ran like a decorative frieze under the eaves along the verandahs all around the house.

The house was an office in which a few Chinese clerks were working. Questioning elicited the information that it served as the office of a rice mill which stood on the adjacent plot of land. Ascending the stairs for further inspection, they arrived at the conclusion that the house was exactly what they wanted, and in fine condition. Some old, broken-down rickshaws and the remains of horse carriages found in the compound bore evidence to the affluence of its past owner.

There were altogether twelve rooms, each one beautifully spacious, not counting the verandahs and the pavilion of the kind called a *sala*. The architect made a rough mental calculation that the main building alone could seat more than a hundred diners, were it to be turned into a restaurant. An old man came up and told them that he was the caretaker, so they asked him how to contact the present owner.

All went well at the start—and the point in time at which they succeeded in negotiating with the heir of the nobleman who had owned the house can well be counted as the beginning of the story.

Even though they had not been able to persuade him to sell the title deed, they did manage to obtain a long-term lease of the property, which was quite satisfactory. It brought the millionaire's project close to reality.

The architect with the western university degree went back again and again in order to make a thorough survey. He visualized how the marble-lined terrace by the river, together with the green house (he subsequently called it "the green mansion"), would appear after it had been renovated and redecorated as a restaurant. Somehow the whole thing seemed to remain incomplete and fall short of the magnificence that he hoped to achieve. In his mind's eye, he envisioned the warm grace and opulence of the bygone past that he so wanted to recreate.

He thought that there was something lacking . . . something still missing, something that would make it a complete whole—as he saw it with his inner eye.

The architect spent several more days pondering before coming to the conclusion that a big Thai house was needed.

And this is exactly where we can pin the blame on the architect.

He did not want a modern Thai house but a genuinely old one. He respected the venerable grace and grave dignity that gave an air of antiquity to the green mansion. He did not want the kind of Thai house that would spoil the mood of the guests who set foot in the compound with the addition of something new and tasteless.

And the Thai house that he wanted was not a Thai house in the sense of a residence, because such a structure would not be suitable for a restaurant, but rather something in the way of a pavilion, like a *sala kan parian*—spacious and open.

The millionaire fell in with the architect's line of thought. The two sent out agents to comb the provinces of Ang Thong, Ayutthaya and Supan Buri for Thai houses in the style of the central plains. Nothing of the kind was to be found. They were to be found only in temples, according to some people.

"Which temples?" No one could answer the millionaire's question.

Meanwhile, the architect had driven northward with a friend. As their car rolled past an old monastery, his eyes caught sight of an aged northern-style structure standing there in the compound. At the architect's request, his friend turned the car into the monastery grounds.

The architect told himself that this was "it". This was precisely what he was looking for.

It was a wooden *sala*, an open pavilion-like structure traditionally used for religious rites by rural monks and lay villagers in the manner of their counterparts in the central region, though it was smaller and without the raised floor. Superficially, the *sala* appeared to be in a dilapidated state. After a brief survey, the architect was convinced that it was strong and complete, despite its lopsided appearance and collection of holes in its roof.

In addition to its fine proportions and spaciousness, the architect was impressed by the finely carved floral-motif gables as well as the lotus molding that formed the capitals of the pillars and the beautiful fretwork that graced other parts of the structure. The important fact was that the whole pavilion was built of solid teak with admirable workmanship.

The architect asked to speak with the abbot and learnt from him that the *sala* was well over a hundred years old. The villagers called it "*Sala* Hoi Khao". The architect then expressed his fears the old *sala* might collapse one the these days while the villagers were gathered in it for some religious ceremonies of merit-making. The elderly abbot agreed, saying that there was nothing he could do as there wasn't enough money to repair it. The architect was able to understand the thoughts and feelings of the old man.

After bidding goodbye to the abbot, he proceeded to photograph the *sala* from every side and at every corner, not forgetting the details of the wood carvings and fretwork that ornamented the building.

The architect returned to Bangkok earlier than scheduled. He enlarged the photographs that he had taken and showed them to the millionaire and all those concerned. He described to them the beauty and the antiquity of the teakwood *sala*. He made sketches to show how it would look if it were to be put together with the green mansion. What he made was a very clear presentation of the way the old *sala* would be joined to the green mansion to make a magnificent riverside restaurant.

It was unanimously agreed that the century-old *sala* would have to be dismantled and brought down to Bangkok.

The saying that money has the power to bring about the realization of one's wishes may be true, but it may not hold for certain places and circumstances. To move this aged, close-to-collapsing *sala* was not as easy as they had thought. There remained villagers who were not completely ignorant and blind to the beauty and the values of old architecture. When the architect returned to the temple for the third or the fourth time, voices of dissent began to make themselves heard.

The man who opposed the move most strongly was named In, a man whom his fellow villagers called "In *Chang*" or "In, the Builder". "In" was the name his parents gave him, "*Chang*" was the indication that he was a builder of houses.

It was surprising that no one called him "*sla*" or craftsman.

In *Chang* was over sixty years old. He had an understandable reason to be against the dismantling of the *sala*—his grandfather had built it with his own hands. Ever since he was born, he had seen this *sala*. He had sat in it, lain on it, walked past it, worked on it—his whole life revolved around it. In fact, he loved it and was more attached to it than to his own house.

The *sala* was grandfather's handiwork. His father had told him this and often repeated it to him. The governor of the province had told his grandfather to build it.

It was his grandfather's work, his father's pride, and In *Chang*'s own heart and mind. This *sala* had put him on his life-path and made him a builder like his father and his grandfather before him. In *Chang*'s father had impressed the fact that it was born out of his grandfather's craftsmanship—it was a fact that had been imprinted in his memory through frequent repetition. In *Chang* had spent his whole life with this *Sala* Hoi Khao. He knew every post, every board, and every motif in all the ornamental designs that enriched it. He had been the sole repairer of this building during all these years . . . and though he had done all he could, the *sala* still looked as if it might soon fall down.

"What if it falls? What if someone dies? What would we do?"

The abbot asked In *Chang*.

"I could mend it, *Tu Pho*. It wouldn't fall." In Chang insisted.

Yes, he was sure that he could repair this *sala* and that it would not fall down.

"How much money would it take to mend it?"

"Where can we find the money?"

To the abbot's last two questions In *Chang* was at a loss to find an answer, as were the five or six villagers who were his fellow dissenters. Money was an essential requirement if the repair was to be done, but where was the money to be found?

Money might not be able to effect every change, but when the money came with the governor of the province, everything was smoother.

The governor was a friend of the millionaire.

Within a few days, the framed and neatly colored plan of the new *sala*, designed by the architect and considerably larger than the old one, was hanging on the wall of the abbot's *kuti*.[1] The governor called a meeting of all the villagers to make an announcement in reference to the age and broken down condition of the century-old *sala*, followed by an assurance that as soon as it was taken down, a larger and more strongly-built *sala* would be put up in its place. The replacement would be completed within three months and would come with the addition of a large Buddha image.

The villagers were happy, but In *Chang* had to turn his face to brush away his tears.

The architect brought workmen all the way from Bangkok. No one wondered why he did not have the *sala* taken apart by the local builders. No one had asked him, but the architect knew in his own heart that he was preventing possibilities of error. If he had used the local builders to take it down, he would have to take them all to Bangkok to rebuild it. According to his plans, it would be his own workmen who dismantled it and would reassemble it later.

The task should not be a difficult one because not a single nail was used in this *sala*.

If there had been one other reason for not using the local craftsmen, it might have been the fact that he had already met In

1. monk's abode, traditionally small and simple

Chang, had known who In *Chang* was, and had sensed In *Chang*'s hurt and sorrow in regard to his beloved *Sala* Hoi Khao. The architect had glimpsed the shining reflection of tears in In *Chang*'s eyes on the day they began to take it apart. The architect had tried not to pay any attention and not to glance in the direction of In *Chang*. If he had allowed the local builders to help, it was certain that In *Chang* was sure to be among them. Looking at it from the point of view of humanity, according to his own ideas, the architect thought that would be inflicting too much unkindness on a rural villager like In *Chang*.

No one thought of the differences between a local builder and a Bangkok one.

Not even In *Chang* himself.

They took apart the components of the *sala* with great care, packed each piece into a box or a crate which was securely fastened with nails prior to being conveyed to Bangkok in three big trucks. For pieces with wood rot, they constructed special boxes to take them either to be repaired or to have replicas made. No part of the *sala* was left behind except for the tiles from the roof. These were scattered in abandoned piles because the architect had already taken a few samples to a ceramic factory in order to make molds from which copies were to be baked using identical forms and colored glaze as the originals.

One month passed. *Sala* Hoi Khao took shape on the bank of the Chao Phraya River. The sight caused no small wonderment in those who saw it from adjacent plots and from passing boats on the river.

This was the one and only of its kind. This was the only restaurant in Bangkok to be able to boast of a beautiful *sala* of the northern Thai architectural style of genuine antiquity. Such magnificent grace and craftsmanship. The architect could not help thinking a somewhat self-congratulatory thought that it had an air of antiquity that went so extraordinarily well with the green mansion. He felt proud that the marble terrace could set off the majesty of the northern-style *sala* and green mansion to such perfection.

Even though they did not know the meaning of *hoi khao*, they continued to call it *hoi khao* just as the villagers had done.

Though there were similarities in the form of *Sala* Hoi Khao and the standard ordination hall of the Department of Religious Affairs, it was notable that *Sala* Hoi Khao was not as tall, wider in proportion, more squat in shape and unencumbered by the busy intricacy of openwork patterns which were usually covered with glittering decorations of mirror mosaics. *Sala* Hoi Khao's roof was double-tiered. The finials, shaped like the mythological serpents called *naga*, pointed straight up at the sky in the architectural style typical of the north, unlike the gracefully curved finials so familiar to the eyes of Bangkokians. They looked stiff but dignified. The slopes of the roof were wide and gentle, one roof tier above the other.

Looking at the *sala* directly from the front or from the rear, one could see four rows of teak pillars. Those in the two center rows which took the weight of the gables were larger than the ones in the two side rows.

There were altogether four pillars that supported the gables and the pediments—two at the front, and two at the rear. They were, like the smaller pillars, standing trunks of teak trees—round, each one large enough to be just encircled by a man's arms. They were entirely without any joints, being the trunks of single trees.

The architect often stood beside these four pillars stroking them with a sense of elation. They were the most beautiful teakwood pillars he had every seen in his life—aged, smooth, gleaming, straight, and round. The lotus motif was carved into the very wood of the pillar. Often, the feel of these venerable columns gave him goose pimples.

In point of fact, he felt like putting his palms together in the traditional *wai* to these four pillars—not in homage to the lumber but to the craftsmen who had carved and turned them to such perfection making the pillars identical in texture, color, smoothess and size.

The publicity campaign for the restaurant was a resounding one. The contruction of *Sala* Hoi Khao was finalized. The gilt on the carved floral motif of the gables and on the blossoms in the openwork around the *sala* gleamed so brightly that it looked as if the whole structure was ornamented with flowers of radiant gold the brilliance of which was further set off by the scarlet of the wooden beams beneath the eaves. The newness of the gold-colored roof tiles sparkled richly with reflections of sunlight. And on nights with a bright moon, there would be a glimmering pool of silvery light in the middle of the roof. The pool of light would shine the brightest on full moon nights.

They—the architect, the millionaire and those who had any hand in it—were proud of this *sala*. Even the stately green mansion was overshadowed. The press began to trickle in for news and interviews, or to take photographs and taste the food. One and all were impressed and full of praise—oh, what a worthwhile investment!.

The millionaire was the proudest of all. He was filled with satisfaction. This was what was needed for the remaining years of his life—not wealth, not honor, but the distinction of being the preserver of a priceless work of architecture by not neglecting its decay.

The inaugural celebration of the restaurant was a grand affair in which *Sala* Hoi Khao played the leading role. Every important guest wanted to be seated in it. And, in keeping with the regional style of the architecture, the softly rhythmic nail dance of the north was performed with melodic interludes of songs from that particular kind of northern guitar called *sung*. Every table was lit by large red candles.

The entertainment in the green mansion was Thai dancing and music of the classical genre. Members of high society turned up in force. Arrangements had been made to convey guests from the parking lot to the riverside by rickshaws and horse carriages.

The opening celebration of the most opulent restaurant on the bank of the Chao Phraya progressed into the night to the great enjoyment of everyone. The architect was the person who received the most credit. He answered endless questions about *Sala* Hoi Khao without a trace of boredom or exhaustion.

In the midst of the festivities, a strange sound could be heard . . . and *Sala* Hoi Khao seemed to sway very slightly. Few noticed the sound or felt the sway. None paid any attention. Some thought the sound was the musician tuning the *sung*, yet others thought that the sway was caused by the impact of a riverine wave on one of the posts or the weight of a heavy truck on the road behind the compound.

The gaiety of the atmosphere and the vivacity of the conversation prevented thoughts of anything more ominous. No one wondered how powerful a wave had to be to cause an impact on such a solid structure, or how a truck could be speeding through a parking lot packed with cars.

The inauguration party passed with great success. The riverside restaurant was as elegant and profitable as anticipated.

One month went by.

No one in the management noted anything unusual but the employees who remained after the closing of the restaurant each night began to noitice certain anomalies. In the stillness of night, they would often hear loud creaking noise like the shrinking of wood in the winter. No one paid much attention at first. But as the sound became more frequent, they began to look at one another with questioning eyes. No one was sure where it came from because it resounded so piercingly throughout *Sala* Hoi Khao and the green mansion.

Sala Hoi Khao swayed frequently but they thought it was only because part of it stood under the water. They failed to realize that it stood on steel and concrete pilings which were driven deep into the river bed and were far too sturdy to be the source of the swaying.

Then it came, late in the silence of the night . . .

While the employees were making their final rounds before retiring to their rest, a long and blood-curdling wail of some unseen thing sounded—from *Sala* Hoi Khao for certain, there was no doubt about it this time because it was very loud and clear—like the twist and breaking of a great piece of wood. Then, all of a sudden, came a high long drawn sound like wood cracking. *Sala*

Hoi Khao shuddered as if shaken by a giant's hand. Roof tiles fell and shattered on the paving. Even the green mansion shook. In a moment, everthing was still.

Everyone was terror-stricken. At first they thought it was an earthquake, but why did it affect only *Sala* Hoi Khao?

The roof was repaired without difficulty. There was no other damage. All the employees were instructed to keep the strictest silence—nothing was to leak out to outsiders.

But the incident went on recurring—it was fortunate that it only occurred after the restaurant was closed for the night. Nevertheless, it grew more and more frequent each night to the point that the millionaire and the architect decided to come and stay overnight in order to investigate the matter—partly because several employees had become so nervous that they refused to remain after work.

And it really happened . . . the noise and the tremor was such that the millionaire and the architect had to rush out of *Sala* Hoi Khao for fear of it collapsing on them.

Then, one night an exorcist from the old city of Ayutthaya, whom we shall from now on call "the witch doctor", came after the nightly closure of the restaurant.

It was the only solution the architect could think of after he had carefully inspected every detail of the structure and could find nothing that could account for the phenomena.

The witch doctor's rite took several hours in an eerie, ghostly atmosphere. As the witch doctor mumbled his myterious mantra while holding a large bunch of lighted incense sticks, a long, hair-raising sound erupted—the same cracking, screeching wail that had become familiar of late but much more drawn out than ever before, so long drawn out that had it been emitted by a human being it would have taken at least two deep breaths to accomplish such a lengthy wail.

The witch doctor said it was the scream of the *takian* ghost, the female ghost who resided in one of the four teak pillars that held up the gables. The words struck deep fear into the hearts of all present, especially because what had gone before seemed to bear evidence to them.

The wailing stopped at the approach of dawn. The witch doctor claimed that he had captured the *takian* ghost. He put the earthenware pot where he had imprisoned it into the cloth bag that he slung over his shoulder, pocketed his fee, and went home. Everyone felt a sense of relief even though the employees continued talking about the whole nerve racking affair with some relish.

While all this was passing in Bangkok, the building of the new *sala* was completed. It was a big concrete *sala*, beautified on all sides with silver-painted iron grilles which enclosed it on all sides. It was no longer the open *sala* that used to stand there in the old days. No matter where one looked, there were the angels with hands held on their chests like lotuses—these angels being the motif of the design of the iron grilles along the sides of the *sala*. These, and the celestial door guardians that were the motif of the grilles at the front and the back.

In *Chang* looked at the *sala* with a desolate heart. He thought of *Sala* Hoi Khao, of the lifework of his grandfather, of the structure of which his father was so proud, of what was like his own life and soul.

The new *sala* was like a stranger from an alien land—someone he didn't know and didn't want to greet or to converse with.

After the witch doctor had captured and taken the *takian* ghost away (according to his claim—he had also declared that he was going to set it free in the forests near Ayutthaya), the strange wailing sounds ceased for two whole days. Everyone was noticeable happier. The architect was relieved; so was the millionaire. The latter, however, was bothered by the increasingly expansive gossip about the power of the *takian* ghost which had not yet reached the public's ear due to various tactics devised by the millionaire himself.

On the third day after the witch doctor's rite, a strange phenomenon occurred—this time at an utterly wrong hour.

It came at about nine o'clock Friday night when *Sala* Hoi Khao was packed with diners and when the waiters and waitresses were at their busiest with orders and dishes.

All of a sudden a long, drawn-out, screeching wail pierced the chattering voices of the diners who, together with the waiters and waitresses, looked up at the ceiling from which the sound seemed to emanate. Silence fell. The sound was heard even by those seated in the green mansion. Silence fell. One by one the diners there also stopped talking. Many unconsciously stroked their own arms on which goose pimples were rising.

After the sound had come to a stop, and someone was just beginning to laugh in the face of the blank silence, the hair-raising sound started all over again. Its loudness was such that it seemed the vast *sala* might crumble all at once. The four big pillars twisted, creaked and swayed in a horrifying manner. The gables, both at the front and the back, screeched for all the world as if pulled by a number of elephants.

Pandemonium broke out. The terrifying sound not only would not stop but grew increasingly louder. The *sala* leaned and settled on the left side. It was filled with noises of chairs falling, and people yelling and screaming in terror. Several diners jumped into the water. Those in the green mansion caught the panic, and everyone rushed out to the riverside terrance or to the parking lot at the back. Many fell and could not regain their feet because of the number of people running past.

The roof tiles fell crashing in every direction as though clawed by a titan. Several people shouted "Earthquake!" If it were so, why did the tremor only affect *Sala* Hoi Khao? The green mansion trembled enough to send dishes falling without any part of the structure being the least damaged.

Though this incident caused no fatalities, it resulted in a good number of injuries, in several cases severe.

The restaurant was closed.

The front and the back of *Sala* Hoi Khao were twisted towards each other by the weight of the inward leaning of two of the large teak pillars. The left side settled in an alarming manner and all the smaller pillars twisted and leaned along with it. The surprising thing was that none of the wood components were broken or fell down though almost no tiles were left on the roof.

The uncanny fact was that the srange noise persisted intermittently, at times in short, broken rhythm that sounded almost like human sobs.

The consensus to dismantle *Sala* Hoi Khao was unanimously reached. Another exorcist and a medium came to perform separate rites at different times without any positive results. The new exorcist insisted that there was no evil spirit of any kind in either *Sala* Hoi Khao or the green mansion. The medium invoked spirits with utter lack of response from any incorporeal beings, at least not until the spirit of a child who had drowned in the river in front of the rice mill came—no one knew how. A long conversation with the child ghost preceded the final realization that it knew absolutely nothing about *Sala* Hoi Khao.

The dismantling of *Sala* Hoi Khao caused deep regrets. Though no one knew what to do after it was accomplished, they knew that the *sala* could not be left as it stood because it could collapse at anytime.

One day before they embarked on dismantling the *sala*, In *Chang* and a few villagers followed the abbot down to Bangkok to buy a Buddha image for their new *sala*—the funds for this purchase being the proceeds of none other than the barter involving *Sala* Hoi Khao. In *Chang* had seen photographs of *Sala* Hoi Khao in the newspaper and had told the abbot that they should go and take a look at their old *sala*—people had been saying that it was haunted and was about to be pulled down because it was on the brink of collapse.

The abbot and the villagers didn't really want to go because they felt it might embrrass the present owner. In fact, the abbot himself felt guilty—it was as if he had taken advantage of the new owner who had built such a grand and lavish new structure for the monastery in exchange for such a derelict, crumbling old building about to be taken down.

But In *Chang* wanted to take a look. Some deep urge was prompting him to go and see his *sala*, his grandfather's *sala*, his father's *sala* —the *sala* that was his very heart and soul.

In *Chang* wanted to know how and why the *sala* was falling down.

In *Chang* missed *Sala* Hoi Khao—and he believed that the *sala* missed him, too. His single-minded determination overrode the others' reluctance. Besides, the abbot had always felt considerable guilt about the barter where In *Chang* was concerned.

In *Chang*, the abbot and the villager friends of In *Chang* arrived at the riverside restaurant in the afternoon when the builders were trying to find the best way to take down *Sala* Hoi Khao. The architect was there, so was the millionaire. Both felt awkward at the sight of the abbot and In *Chang*—part of the awkwardness was embarrassment. They couldn't quite explain why, nor who embarrassed them more, the abbot or In *Chang*.

They invited the abbot to take a seat and told him the story.

In *Chang* looked at *Sala* Hoi Khao. He gazed sorrrowfully at the *sala* of his heart and life. It wouldn't have come to this if it had remained in the monastery. It wouldn't have been so bent and twisted. In *Chang* walked round and round the *sala*, touching every pillar, every openwork panel that he passed. He felt such sorrow for the *sala* that his eyes brimmed over with tears. He thought of his grandfather, of his father—of how his grandfather used to touch, his father used to stroke, every pillar and every panel, just as In *Chang* himself always did. Every lovingly-carved flower was like a long-loved friend or a deeply-revered relative.

The *sala* was nearing its end. They were dismembering it, and it was most likely that it would not ever be assembled again. In *Chang* thoughtfully felt the grains of the pillars with his fingers, his eyes shining with tears; but when his hand touched the big pillars that leaned low inward at the front of the *sala*, In *Chang* sensed that something was wrong. He walked around towards the back and stroked the other big pillar that leaned and twisted inward. He ran his palm up and down the pillar before quickly making his way to the abbot.

"The pillars are paired wrong, *Tu Pho* !"

Excitedly, In *Chang* told the abbot that the big pillars were paired wrongly. The architect didn't quite catch what he said. He looked at In *Chang* with genuine sympathy. He was a craftsman himself, so was In *Chang*—therein lay his respect for this villager.

He had never looked down on the fact that In *Chang* was a rural builder. At this moment he actually felt ashamed of In *Chang*—definitely more ashamed of In *Chang* than of the abbot.

"We are going pull it down, Uncle," he said sadly to In *Chang*—mainly because he was at a loss to find anything else to say.

"Yes, take it down . . . ," In *Chang* told the architect, " . . . and put it up again with the pillars paired rightly."

"Why, Uncle? Are the pillars paired wrongly? But what difference does it make?" The architect felt a rising excitement.

"They have stood together for a hundred years, how can you have the heart to go and separate them?"

In *Chang* replied with a tremor in his voice and tears running down his cheeks, as he turned to look at *Sala* Hoi Khao with an inexpressible pity spreading through the depths of his heart.

MOTHER!

ANCHAN

Translated by Kuruvin Boon-long

MY mother died two nights ago.

The white half-curtain stretched across the wooden bars of the window at the foot of my bed still bears the hole made by my fingers that are forever looking for mischief. Machine-embroidered in a cut-work pattern of a rabbit surveying the moon, it was bought only last Saturday when we went to Phahurat [1] together.

I can still hear you threatening to smack me hard if I did it again. And you know what, Mummy? I've done it again. And guess where your black curlers are, they and what was once a biscuit tin that you were frantically looking for the other day. I took them and pretended they were wheels of a steam roller. All of them. And then I left them under the mango tree behind the house, and they got rained on. That was only three or four days ago.

I can remember you cuddling me there, and rocking me to the rhythm of our very own secret song. It's a song that came to me all of a sudden. You liked it when you first heard me sing and laughed when you saw me dance to it, so much that your body

---

1. Indian quarter in Bangkok famous for its textile trade

rocked back and forth. But when your fingers that reached out to stroke my hair came upon bits of earth I had scooped up and sprinkled myself with, your mood changed. You started to shout, saying that you've never come across a child as naughty as me. My singing turned to sobs but still you said you would beat me to death if I didn't stop crying. And you made me go and have a bath.

When my bath was over, I stole into the the loo, grabbing a leaf of the jack fruit tree to wipe my bottom with. It was you who told me that I was a grown-up and must learn to wash my own bottom. You came over and, sensing something was amiss, made to smack me while trying to hold back your smile, and washed my bottom for me, as you always did.

I wonder if you've now found out that I was the culprit that picked the baby jack fruits. I'd pick some every time I picked their leaves. I blamed the bats and you believed me and were cross with them. It was me, Mum. I was naughty again.

All through this night I lie alone on the big bed, my eyes wide open. Open for no particular reason. I'm lying right on the spot where you always slept, my head resting on the pillow you've always used. I'm not crying, not doing anything. To me you're special, too special to cry for and thus relieve the pain, like the hundreds of people that I know would have done.

Everyone has gone to the temple to be with you. Everyone except Grandma and a few who stayed behind because of me. Because *Lung Mo* [2] Lek told them not to take their eyes off me. Grandma loves me just the way you loved me but her heart knows nothing of the little secrets that I've hidden away in the nooks and crannies of our home. Nothing of the unimaginable trove of treasures that the pirates have hidden behind the kitchen, nor Dora-emon's favorite hiding place by the side of the cupboard. Dora-emon, the clever cat that can ease his way from between the pages of my comic books to play chase with me. And he even knows how to play without me having to tell him.

2. *Lung*, "uncle", and *mo*, "doctor", are the titles used to address Lek. He may be either a real uncle or a close family acquaintance.

Then there's the biggest secret of all, hidden in the rattan handbag and kept under the bed. You guarded it so jealously but even you couldn't stop the mischief within me from finding it. I had to crawl under the bed to get it out and inside there were pictures of a good-looking man. Two or three pictures of someone, stowed deep inside the bag. This was the only secret that I didn't dare ask you about, even though I've often cried and begged you to go and buy me a father instead of that teddy you brought home for me.

The light of the full moon filters through the embroidered holes of the half-curtain, turning into dancing shadows in the mirror. You loved to sing and dance more than anybody. You often burst into your tuneless singing regardless of the time of day. There were times when I caught you singing and dancing quietly by yourself in front of that mirror. But when you spotted me, you stopped and laughed bashfully. I remember it all.

Tonight, all I have are those shadows. My heart feels so tight. The half-curtain hangs still. My heart skips a beat. A breeze wafts its way in and the half-curtain sways. Bright moonbeams find their way into the room and the shadows again come to life, and I feel as though you're dancing next to me. All these feelings are growing stronger as I wait for you to cuddle me close and let me cry into your lap. I feel the start of a shuddering sob for want of you. I want to let it all come out but I shall hold my tears for when you come back. I will cry them all then and make you feel so awful for keeping me waiting.

Click!

The sound of a light switch being turned on. The room is bright with light and the shadows have disappeared. I stop my sobbing and quickly turn to face the wall. Grandma has come to check on me again. I'm really fed up with Grandma.

"Nui. Nui love. I've got some rice soup for you and *mu-yong* [3] as well. Come on, quick!" I turn away from the soup bowl. I don't even want to talk, let alone eat. So I shake my head to try and escape my grandma's hand, but she isn't going to give up easily.

3. a kind of sweet, shredded dried pork

"Come on, I'll feed you. Um! Open your mouth, my precious . . ." And it's her that can't stop the tears from falling even though she's only just come in looking all bright and cheerful. I eat a few mouthfuls to get it over and done with so she will stop fussing over me. But it looks as though I've made her happy because she manages to smile through her tears. Grandma quickly walks over to the window and flips up the half-curtain, letting a breeze in to ease the hot stillness. She then picks up the bowl and takes it to the kitchen. I'm on my own again.

As soon as Grandma's back is turned, I jump out of bed, switch off the light and climb back in to lie still in the darkness. Only my eyes move, following the shadowy shapes of branches of the champak tree outside my window. Shadows that move and dance on the floor in front of the mirror. The scent of the champak flowers filled the room as soon as Grandma flipped up the half-curtain but I was oblivious to the smell. Everything in me is concentrated in front of that mirror.

Oh, Mum! What must I do to see you again? I promise never to make a hole in that curtain. Never to play with your curlers and then lose them. Never to pick the young jackfruits off the tree. And never ever again to bring out those pictures that you loved. Mum, please come back to me. Please, Mum!

My eyelids grow heavy.

The darkness behind those closed lids is so enveloping that I have to quickly open them. My heart hammers loudly but it soon calms down when I see the shadows still on the floor, gyrating companionably.

I often have nightmares and you of all people know this. Many a time have I woken up whimpering because I've been frightened by the ghosts inside my eyes. And you would turn over to hug and kiss me over and over and comfort me back to sleep. You would tell me that I needn't be afraid as long as you were by my side, and I would obediently close my eyes.

The next thing I knew I found myself sitting all alone on some roots, digging up sand. I didn't know where you'd gone. There was just me beside that gigantic trunk of an ancient tree, so old that its

48

bark had turned to coarse stone. Its branches, gnarled and twisted, stretched over the vast chasm that plunged steeply down. It was a solitary tree, perched precariously on the edge of that parched precipice.

I craned my neck to see into the depth and my eyes lighted on the distant sea and the silent stretch of sand at the foot of the rock face. I talked myself into believing that this was like the times when I had played on the beaches in Cha-am, but something inside told me that this was different. The sea was not its usual indigo but turgid, black, and unfathomable, void of movement, not even a hint of a wave. The whole scene was deathly still and breathless.

All around me the sand was blighted by roots pushing up in an untidy fashion. They surfaced and tangled before disappearing deep into the ground, worming their way to surface yet again but I knew not where.

Suddenly I felt so afraid of this place that I stopped my play and hurriedly climbed the branches of the tree. I thought that when I got to the top I would find a haven of safety amongst its arms. But as soon as my hands caught hold of the branch that hung over the chasm, the tree shook alarmingly all over as if to uproot itself.

In a flash, the wide open sea below started to moan as if the ocean floor had been wrenched apart, leaving a deep gaping hole that sucked down the sea water with such force and speed that soon all that remained were the drying pebbles on the sea-bed.

In that split second it dawned on me that the tree I had climbed was an opening to a door that had been sealed closed. Its roots reached deep and embedded themselves under the sea floor, preventing whatever was underneath from escaping. By touching that branch, I had set off the tremor that traveled down to the tips of the roots holding that door closed. So strong was the force that the sea floor burst open like a deep wound in the earth.

I gripped the branch with both hands while my body dangled in space over the chasm. It was then that I screamed. Looking down, I had seen the ghoul watching me from its deep abode. I didn't see its face clearly because it was a very long way down but

I could see that it was smiling and its hands were reaching up, higher and higher. I screamed again and thrashed about in the air, afraid that its hands might reach me and pull me down. If that happened, I knew that I would never wake again when the dawn came.

In my dream I struggled to open my eyes and wake myself but I couldn't. Then I saw you, Mum. I didn't know how long you had been there but there you were with a ladder. You leaned it against the tree and scaled the rungs as if you knew that you must not touch certain parts of that strange tree. I also saw my brown teddy undoing the red polka dot ribbon from his neck and binding the ladder to the tree with it so that you could get to me quickly. I heard the sound of loud, excited hand-clapping all around me and all the time the ghoul's hands shrank further from me, now in your embrace. You dried my eyes and carried me to Teddy who set me down to wait for you on the ground. You had picked up a magic sword, made out of an eraser, and cut down the ghoul with all your might. Wherever the sword cut, that ghoulish part would disappear just as a pencil mark on a piece of paper would when rubbed with a good rubber, every mark until all that remained was a clean sheet of paper, free of all things menacing.

I heard the gurgle of water and saw the sea gushing out from the orifice to replenish itself. You gave me a piggy-back ride down the rock face to the beach below. You then took something else out of your rattan bag, this time a big box of crayons and we proceeded to color the sea the bluest of blues with the crayon that I chose. Meanwhile Teddy was puffing his cheeks and blowing, dissipating the big waves into small ripples which chased each other to the shore. Ripples for you and I to splash happily in. Before we left, we crayoned in flowers and leaves for that naked tree till it was covered in the brightest shades of red, yellow, and green yielded by my box. I turned for one last look before pulling you away and the beauty of it stuck to my mind, like a magic picture.

When I woke the next morning and questioned you about the past night, you took to scolding me, saying it was a nonsensical dream. But when I looked into your eyes, I knew, and I pestered you all through the day till it was time again for bed. It was then that you let me into the secret. You said that this would be our biggest secret and no one else knew about it, not even Grandma. You said that even if the infinite sky separated us, the love that existed between mother and child would cover that distance and bring us together. You gave me the box of crayons that we used the previous night and told me to draw whatever came to my mind should you happen to be away from me one day.

That was all you said and you stroked my cheek and scratched my back till I grew drowsy and we slept close together, every night. No matter how often I stirred, the perfume of your talc which you smoothed over your body before going to bed would lull me back to slumber, like a sleepy child rocked in its cradle to the lullaby brimming with its mother's boundless love.

Now I must be brave and close those eyes, all on my own.

I see the vast darkness so clearly behind my closed lids, it's like seeing it in the light of day. The ring of darkness begins to fade like water stains that spread on a piece of paper which has been dipped in black paint and then sponged till it turns a dull grey. It's like a dull grey blanket that hangs damp and drab, it's like taking cover from the rain by leaning against a clammy rotting wall through which water has seeped, leaving a musty stale odour. I come to the conclusion that if loneliness and being afraid were to be a color, it wouldn't be any other color but this.

Instantly I see that same ghoul floating towards me. Its mouth is in the throes of soundless laughter, as if in a silent movie. This embellishes its movements, making it all the more terrifying. I see one of its eyes rolling, and moving through the air to keep up with its teeth.

Before I can blink, the other eyeball joins its partner and forms an ill-defined face of unimaginable hideousness. Although my eyes are closed, I am fully awake so what I see is no figment of my imagination.

It's come back for me, that's for sure, because it was outwitted by you the last time. It must have found out that from tonight, I am without you. I try to open my eyes knowing that it can only come into being behind my eyelids. As long as I can keep them from closing, whatever lies behind those lids will not bother me.

The breeze that sways the champak tree and creates dancing shadows in front of the mirror suddenly drops. Outside the sounds of insects hush to a silence. The scent of the champak palls and the moon begins pushing its way behind a dark cloud. But the fireflies become more profuse, shimmering in the clumps of foliage in the depth of the garden. The more I look, the more they remind me of the eyes of *krasoes* [4] keeping an interminable watch.

I try calling for Grandma but the sound won't come. Grandma who came in so often to check on me, where is she now? Why isn't she here? If it can put together its head and body that Mum rubbed off, and reach me with its long arms, that would be it, and who would Grandma have to live with then?

The hours pass and I grow more sleepy. The moon slowly sails from behind the cloud to shine its light. The breeze picks up and sways the branches of the champak tree till they sigh and shadows return to the floor, their movements dependent on the breeze. They move close to the top of my bed seeming to enjoy their song and dance. As the singing crescendoes, I start to see the hues of sunlight, the colors of flowers in full bloom. I suddenly think of my box of crayons and it materializes before me, open to display the shades of the rainbow. My heart settles on a sweet pink and, with my eyes closed, I begin drawing you. It's a race against time. The ghoul has rebuilt itself and, with its long hand, grabs my crayon even though your picture isn't finished. I haven't even drawn your hands that they might hold me and hide me behind your back. Then you start to sing our song and you smile and nod for me to conduct the musical notes that tumble out of your mouth like a cascade of water. The notes dance themselves into rows like soldiers and the room resounds with melodious harmony made by the army of music with you as its general. Countless notes line up to form a chain which move in to fetter the ghoul while their reinforcements clamber on and completely cover the specter.

4. terrifying, female ghouls

Every note joins in the singing and the whole room reverberates with your song.

When the music around me has abated like water that has run its course, I stop my crying and spy two ping-pong balls in the same place where those ghoulish eyes had been. Where its arms were, I see the two new paint brushes that I've begged to have. I dash out to find the pink crayon that was knocked out of my hand and fling myself on to you to finish off that hand and make you whole with all that is in me.

And then I cry the locked-away tears which burst out as soon as I find myself in your powdered embrace. We hug each other tight as if nothing matters then, not even death. You cry and then smile before telling me your last secret. You say that whenever I want you, you will be there. I will find you in the words and rhythm of the songs that I sing, in the ABCs that I write, in the sketches that I draw, and in the plasticine that I love to mold. You say that you will be right here, in my small but immeasurably imaginative heart.

Click!

The light switch has been turned on and the room is awash with light. I open my eyes and see Grandma parting the mosquito net to look in at me.

"Gran, Grandma, I'd like some Ovaltine."

With that, I fling myself at her and she holds me close, her tears spilling down onto my cheeks. She keeps shouting to the people outside the room.

"Nit, Nit! Nui's said something. Phone *Mo* Lek first thing tomorrow morning and let him know that Nui has spoken."

GRANDMA sniffs the air and looks as though she's about to say something but changes her mind and sits still for a long time. The scent of the powder floats towards her, its perfume completely eclipses that of the champak. I gently snuggle up to her and within seconds I am fast asleep, my cheeks streaked by Grandma's tears.

THE BEGGARS

ANCHAN

Translated by Chancham Bunnag

AT daybreak the monk walked down the lane accepting food and other offerings from the devotees. As dawn turned into morning, making his way back to the monastery, the monk passed a pair of beggars—man and wife—moving unsteadily along at the start of their begging day. The monk's metal bowl was full and heavy, the beggars' plastic bowl empty. Thus they encountered one another nearly every morning, and the monk often wished to share the food in his bowl with the beggars. He had never done it, though. It would be overreacting to the situation, the monk thought. People would look; it would be embarrassing, he thought.

They met again this morning, like other mornings, but not quite. The monk sensed something different was about to happen. The beggars were standing under the awning in front of a shop-house with the grill-door locked as it was not yet opening time. They looked strangely furtive, the monk thought. A few steps forward and now he could see they were staring hard at him and whispering to each other. Covertly glancing at them, he quickened his pace, meaning to get past the spot where they were lurking as soon as possible. But no longer had he done so than the beggar's wife dashed after him. Now she stood confronting him, barring his path.

The lane this morning was rather quiet, with only a few people going off to work and a few scavenging dogs among the dustbins.

The monk remained stock still, unable to keep his eyes from the woman's hand, which was clutching something inside the grimy cloth bag hanging from her shoulder. He was also wondering how to get away. But at that moment the woman turned and went back to her husband, leaving the monk to hesitate whether to wait or be on his way. He did not hesitate long, steeped as he was in the discipline of monkhood and well-versed in the precept and practice of self-control. He waited and watched calmly as the woman helped her husband—her limping one-legged husband with the crutch—come towards him. The hand inside the bag was twitching as if on the point of taking out whatever it might be. Might it be a knife, perhaps? the monk speculated. Well, if it were, I am young and strong enough to deal with it.

Now it came. Out and up it came. In a flash. No, not a knife. A small plastic bag it turned out to be, securely tied with elastic band and containing plain boiled rice. The woman held it carefully with both hands, raised it to her forehead in a highly respectful gesture, then took her husband's hands to join hers in presenting the bag to the monk.

"Please accept it, Venerable Sir." It was the wife who made the proclamation. They looked timid, awkward and at the same time vigorously determined in their act of giving. The monk blinked in pity at the dirty fingernails before him, then opened his bowl as he would to any other followers of the Lord Buddha, the well-dressed as well as the unwashed. The beggars could see there was virtually no room left in the bowl but with their ill-tended hands managed to squeeze their gift of boiled rice into it.

The monk uttered the usual words of blessing, which were greeted with joyous smiles and several awkward *wais*[1] of reverence and gratitude.

The monk left them and continued on his way. At first his mind was still on the beggars. Having blessed them he now

1. The act of placing hands together palm to palm and raising them to the face.

concentrated on extending to them the beneficence of *metta*—of compassion, of loving kindness. After a while he started to mumble a Pali phrase to himself: *Sabbhe Satta Avera Hontu.* May all beings be free from vengefulness towards one another.

And then the monk went on silently praying and wishing to himself. I have offered loving kindness to the poor needy mendicants. May this meritorious karma be a strengthening factor to guide me to the Sublime Dhamma and that in future I may reach it and become an enlightened one. Here the monk paused for an instant, somewhat abashed by this lofty aspiration, before going on nevertheless with his praying and wishing.

Should my good deed of the mind towards my unfortunate fellow beings like the beggars become part of the pile of merit which, like a bridge, may help me to cross the never-ending whirlpool of suffering and arrive at arahantship—ah, that would be bliss indeed. *Sadhu!*

The eyes of the begging couple followed the monk's progress until he disappeared from sight. They knew not what went on in his mind. They only knew that their earned merit tied to the bag of plain boiled rice was theirs as the bag traveled on in the monk's bowl among other good people's offerings.

"Took your time, didn't you?" the husband was criticizing the wife. "Took your time making up your slow mind. He nearly went past us. How silly you were!"

"Well, I felt ashamed," the wife made her excuse in a small voice. "We only had the rice to give and nothing else. Not even one side dish to go with the rice. It looked ridiculous."

The day wore on. The sun rose higher, hotter. Our monk and the other monks who had been accepting gifts and blessing the givers on this particular morning had returned to their respective monasteries. The two beggars, hand in hand as it were, had gone to settle themselves at their usual place of business located on the pavement almost opposite the entrance to the lane. The wife with her *ching*—a pair of small hand-cymbals—would soon produce the simple rhythm to accompany her husband's singing, for this duet performance was their service to the passersby from whom they hoped to receive a fee in return. The rendition might not be all that melodious but it was a service nonetheless, and the passing audience were perfectly free to pay or not to pay for it. No exploitation of any kind in this exchange.

The husband's song invoked the names of various trees: the *phikun*, the *ket*, the *kaew*, the *satu*, the *sadao*, the crinkly, large-leaved *yang*. He sang of branches and fruit sprouting, sprawling, sparkling, swinging, swerving, swaying, swirling, and so on . . .

The song, all liltingly alliterative, had become quite well known to frequent users of this pavement. The singer enjoyed inserting trills and frills here and there to show off his skill in vocally manipulating the words and the tune. He sang it regularly to his wife's ching-chab, ching-chab beat from her hand cymbals. It could be called their theme song, an indispensable core of their business conducted from morning till evening, everyday. No holidays except when he or she was indisposed. In that case both would be absent from the scene, for one would be ministering to the other at their private abode within walking distance from here.

They could be sitting under the venerable spreading tamarind tree nearby, but chose to expose themselves to the sun in order to be the first to attract the attention of customers. For they did have a few rivals in this neighborhood.

And in this neighborhood the people called them *Ta Kut*—Grandpa Stump—and *Yai Lae*—Grandma Cross-eyed. No doubt the names on their identity cards were different, but would perhaps be considered inappropriately pretty by their fellow citizens who preferred to identify them by their physical defects. It would seem that the nicknames came more easily to the lips.

The couple sat on old newspapers or sometimes empty cement bags, their legs neatly tucked under their buttocks. Not far from their workplace were to be found a popular coffee shop and several stalls selling rice-and-curry, noodles, alcoholic and non-alcoholic drink, roasted this and that, et cetera. Easy to be seen before them on the ground was their plastic begging bowl. Once upon a time it had been a receptacle made from coconut husk. The plastic bowl, a comparatively recent development, was of an unnameable

57

color as it was covered in dust and dirt from the environment, from hands and from coins—coins given out of kindness and pity, or because the donors wished to get rid of cumbersome weight, or from some other reasons beyond the recipients' imagination.

Some parents passing this way liked to make moralistic use of the beggars' infirmities, pointing them out to their five- or six-year-old children while ascribing them—the infirmities—to some bad deeds committed by their owners in the past. If you behave badly to your parents you may end up like Grandpa Stump and Grandma Cross-eyed. That's the gist of the moral. A mother this morning was prattling on this theme to her little daughter, who was thinking: My mother talks too much. I wish she were dumb and couldn't hurt my ear with this awful loud noise. When they had gone past the beggars the little girl turned her head to look at them. Look at them, her mother had said, so now she was looking. She found them fascinating. They're like dolls, thought the little girl. One doll singing, the other going ching-chap ching-chap. *Sanuk!*—quite fun really.

The beggars could never rely on their clientele. Some walked by unfeelingly, indifferently, taking their songs as an integral part of nature, like pouring rain and thunder and lightning. Other strollers, chatting with their loved ones, would dearly opt for more peace and quiet. Still others much preferred the singing to the blasting from motorcyclists—so damn noisy, these would-be speed demons!

But the two beggars could rely on meeting all kinds of human beings in their clientele—every age, sex, profession, attitude. And they had their regular admirers as well: some freelance artists who tippled together in the coffee shop chatting about life and art and whatnot. With their unique eyesight, these artists saw beauty in what might strike others as deplorable. For them poverty on facial expressions and poverty on ragged clothes shone forth in a most appealing way. They even thought it might give them a taste of something deliciously rare to become beggars for a day—when the bowl is filled with coins and the pavement not too hot or too wet. To pass from morning to afternoon to evening without having to look at a watch. No watch to go wrong and needing repair, as a matter af fact. And personal hygiene? Well, there is water to wash that you don't have to pay for. How straightforward, how basic, how uncomplicated life can be. Surrounded by the myriad problems of the well-to-do, beggars are oblivious to them. Beggars are free . . .

The artists were moved by these thoughts and feelings, and transmitted them onto the canvas. They were inspired, to put it simply. They produced some pleasing pictures resulting from this inspiration and the pictures sold quite well. One of them featured Grandma Cross-eyed: the light of the late afternoon, not too glaring, nor yet too dusky, falling mellow and serene on Grandma Cross-eyed of the picture; the venerable tamarind shimmering in the background, Grandma holding herself like a dignified court lady, her eyes fixed on the pair of cymbals in her hands, eyes emitting the disciplined, dedicated look of a musical instructor . . . In reality, Grandma Cross-eyed, with her impaired sight, occasionally missed the target and failed to bring together the two haves of the instrument. Well-aware of her weakness, she concentrated with all her might in order to overcome it, hence that dedicated look, which gave her and, through her, the picture itself, a poignancy that perhaps would not have been there otherwise.

Sometimes a few writers dropped by and were welcomed by our artists. These writers belonged to a radical group whose idealism consisted in their desire to stamp out poverty in this world. Our artists, who jealously treasured their Grandpa Stump and Grandma Cross-eyed, did not want the writers to come tampering with the poverty in this specific spot and didn't even want to discuss the couple with them.

But one day one of the writers—a bearded type, cutting quite an impressive figure—turned up with a book entitled *Beggars*. The picture on the front cover showed under the huge title a cluster of out-sized sinister hands dropping coins into a coconut husk held aloft by a miserable looking creature, a tiny thing dominated and dwarfed by those sinister hands. The grinning writer shyly said that the book had just won an important literary prize, which should bring him a measure of fame. Asked what the book was about he said (a bit bashfully) that it reflected problems having to do with injustice among the people of this land, this society. No matter, the other said, let's drink to it anyway. So, a party got started in celebration of the literary prize mixed with a great deal of good-humoured teasing and pulling the author's leg for the fun of it. The author finally admitted that he found his raw material for the book from this neighborhood. He nodded in the direction of our Grandpa and Grandma, who were singing their song in their habitual unperturbed, untouched-by-extraneous-events manner.

"Those two are my cast of characters," the author quietly said.

"Why didn't you invent a daughter? Give her the *so-u*[2] to play. Then make her become a prostitute and get lots more sympathy for your story." This was contributed by a drinking pal, but nobody paid any attention to him. The party went on. Everybody got drunk and did not go home till very late.

Yes, all kinds of customers and non-customers came and went near where our Grandpa Stump and Grandma Cross-eyed had their place of business.

Once in a while there would come a scrapping couple—scrapping couples were not hard to find in these parts, haranguing in blaring voices that could be heard up and down the lane. These with their surly faces would walk past our Grandpa and Grandma without glancing at them, for they did not want to be reminded that Grandpa Stump, when the sun was scorching, would shield his wife from it with his bedraggled hat. Grandpa did not appear to mind having the fierce sun beating down on himself.

Another familiar sight was Grandpa using the same hat to protect Grandma from getting overly wet on rainy days. When it was merely drizzling gently both of them would sometimes expose themselves and the clothes on their bodies to the cooling water, letting themselves and their clothes be made cleaner at the same time.

Sometimes, while sheltering from the rain under a shopkeeper's eaves, they would hear footsteps approaching and then, in defiance

2. a kind of string instrument

of the deafening downpour, would burst into song to greet prospective customers.

One of the songs brought out a list of animals—the peacock, the deer, the porcupine, the gaur, the bear, the pig. Their names and their movements are intertwined and woven into a rhythmic pattern, in traditional alliterative style that pays more heed to sound than sense but all the same is capable of achieving humour and drama, albeit in a seemingly haphazard way. The deer in the song, for instance, gets his partner pregnant and then leaves her, and we the listeners are asked to grieve with the heartbroken female of the species.

At a certain moment on this particular day, something untoward happened. Perhaps the song upset the customer. In any case the plastic bowl suffered a kick. It went somersaulting and the coins spilled out all over. Grandpa Stump looked up and saw a pretty young girl with a fair complexion. She was hugely pregnant and behind her walked the aged Chinese butcher from the market carrying a parasol to keep the sun from her. Grandpa Stump giggled—what else could he do—and set about putting the scattered coins back into the bowl, thinking: if she wants to vent her frustration on the bowl, let her. And I wonder, he kept on thinking with some amusement about both the Chinese and the young child-girl with very fair skin. Suppose she gives birth to a dark-skinned baby . . . what are you going to do, you Chinese Grandpa? You are a very old man with a hanging, flabby tummy. Where have you found this child to make your mistress? You crave young melons. That's not good for your sagging tummy . . .

A twenty-story condominium rose from the main road on a corner of this lane, soaring higher than the flying kites sent up by the merrily squealing children. This was a wide and longish lane, winding and branching out and then at last becoming no longer a lane but a piece of land featuring a garbage hill, which could also be called a high-rise structure. A slum of sorts had sprung up around here, with our Grandpa and Grandma Beggar among the residents therein. There was also a vacant lot defined by barbwire fences, then a railroad track, and beyond the track an expanse of fields that had not yet been converted into townhouses. The fenced vacant lot belonged to the city administration. The fact that it had been left unbuilt was like playing a joke on those who must squeeze and huddle together in the nearby slum. However, this vacant lot, and especially in the rainy season, was rich in many kinds of wild vegetation such as the *krathin* and the *tamlung*, commonplace, tasty, nutritious stuff. So it was not surprising that much of the fence had fallen to the ground, trampled by the people, who naturally wanted to get through to what Mother Nature so very nicely provided for them.

Grandpa Stump and Grandma Cross-eyed lived not far from the hill of the garbage dump. A not overlarge shed, but commodious enough to allow the two of them to sleep without having to contort themselves. A tin roof, with some holes in it, wobbly wooden posts, a wall made from scraps of this and that salvaged from the dump and other sources, screens taken from torn mats, magazines, posters. What a sense of color, what a sensational collage style, said a student of interior decoration to himself going past the whole effect one sunny day.

From this colorful shed, the old couple with their infirmities took off at the same time as the crowing of the cocks, and returned to it together with the birds coming home at sunset, carrying some plain boiled rice with soy sauce for an evening meal. (During Chinese New Year festivities the owner of the shop often gave them duck or chicken necks to go with the rice.)

And during the day there were plenty of happenings up and down the road and lane for the old couple and their fellow citizens. Transport alone made it a perpetual show: from trucks to motorcycles to wheelbarrows to bicycles to homemade toy vehicles made of empty milk tins and, not least, luxurious passenger cars, whose occupants' eyes would at times meet with the pedestrians' when darkened windows were lowered.

Grandpa Stump and Grandma Cross-eyed were used to gazing at most makes of expensive cars traveling this way, but now, this afternoon, they were thrilled to see something much greater than any routine smart car. Well, it was much, much smarter, it was sleeker, shinier, more blazing, more unusually-shaped, more like a machine in a modern fairy tale movie they had seen on the outdoor screen at a temple fair. This super ultra thing had emerged regally from the lane into the road, the horn screaming imperiously at the song and the cymbal. Barrows and baskets and bamboo poles were quickly shifted to make room for it and yet the young man behind the wheel, winding down the heavily-tinted window, still shouted out warning words like "Hey you, aren't you afraid you'll be run over?"

There was another car parked in front of the young man's super model, so he had to wait in any case, window still down. This gave Grandma Cross-eyed a chance to stare at the girl on the seat beside him. Oh! Grandma exclaimed silently to herself, what a beautiful girl you are, my dear. I've never seen such perfect white skin. Why, you are gorgeous, you are flawless, my little one! Then this beauty turned and glanced at Grandma. The two pairs of eyes met and held. The girl's face had been expressionless, but now she suddenly looked most interested. She said something to the young man. He frowned. She turned back to Grandma and beckoned to her to come forward. Grandma went to the window smiling awkwardly. The girl then gave Grandma a five hundred-baht note, saying not a word. Grandma could smell the cool conditioned air and the lovely scent before the window went up and the car moved on. The lovely scent was gone and in its stead were the powerful fumes left by the car. But Grandma did not notice them as she was still dazed by what had happened.

A few moments after the car had left, people started telling one another about the incident. Did you see it? Five hundred baht she gave to Grandma. She's a star, you know, the most popular singer, just came out with a new tape, best-selling of course. Imagine . . .

Grandpa Stump and Grandma Cross-eyed found themselves the center of attention and enjoyed it immensely.

"That's it, that's it." Grandma was laughing. "Now I remember. I even have the page from the magazine with her picture. Now I remember who she is. I pasted it on the wall, you know."

Now she was showing off her five hundred-baht note to the crowd.

"Why didn't you take down the car's number?" Grandpa Stump teased her in a merry voice. "We could have bought the same number lottery ticket. Might have won plenty."

"Go on talking," said Grandma, "but just don't try to sweet-talk me into giving you my money." Grandma could not stop laughing. "Five hundred," she murmured to the purple note in her hand, fingering it as though wishing to give it life. In her heart she was wishing the girl more wealth, more happiness, more success. You are so famous, my dear and yet you think of a poor beggar by the roadside. Grandma was filled with pleasure thinking of the girl and of the long list of things to buy with this big money. Fish sauce to start with! Delicious fish sauce. Bottles of it! And yes, oh yes, Grandma smiled, side dishes to go with the rice when I offer food to a monk. Grandma looked at her cymbals. They looked newer and glossier than on other days, didn't they?

That exceedingly expensive automobile, after leaving Grandpa Stump and Grandma Cross-eyed's lane, made its way towards the route that would take its passengers to a seaside resort. "I worry about you, Mi," the young man said. "You are always doing crazy things."

"What is so crazy about giving myself a birthday present by giving a present to another? What a pity you didn't see the old woman's eyes when she saw the five hundred-baht note. Oh, Pat, you should have seen it. It is so true, so natural. I would have given a million baht to get that expression. You should have had a camera ready to preserve it for me, to show me how to do it when I have to be in front of the camera." The girl went on and on, her voice growing more vehement, more aggressive, so the man relented and merely chuckled at her finely wrought emotional tray that seemed able to catch and retain every little mood and feeling dropping into it.

"It's wonderful," the girl was saying, "a sum of *only* five hundred can become a sum as *enormous* as five hundred. It depends on who has it—how amazing!"

Now the girl stared out the dark window, not at the view but at the vision of her clothes back home, her clothes and shoes and bags and jewelry and other accessories of all shapes and sizes, some of which had never been worn, some had not even been unpacked since the day they had been whimsically purchased. She drank in her possessions like people who drink water without tasting it because of its indispensability to life.

"It's so marvellous to have money," the man chuckled again, following her sentimental musing. "When one feels like being a saint one spends money and presto, one feels like a saint. Good feelings instantly bought like canned goods in the supermarket. My dear Mi, you take unfair advantage of the rest of us. *So let her be rich and pay for it*, as the Carabao[3] song would put it."

"Don't be silly," the girl glared at him, reaching out a hand to hit him. He averted her attack, then turned on a tape of a gentle sweet tune that after a while easily succeeded in lulling the girl into a dreamy state. She moved her head sleepily; she let the music enter and absorb her being. The man could see that. He was rather fed up with her lightning mood swings, half-censorious of it but as always, could not resist her utterly lovable childlike charm. The car was now on the highway, comfortably passing rural canals and fields, leaving behind the beggars and other people in the smoke of the city.

Before closing her eyes the girl said in a soft voice: "But it's really a very good thing . . . that some awfully poor people do exist."

"And make themselves useful for being poor," the man cut in, glad for the opportunity to be sarcastic.

"Silly!" the girl cried, resorting to her favorite exclamation, but this time with an embarrassed smile on her lips.

3. a popular modern folk group of musicians whose songs address contemporary social issues

65

PEOPLE ON THE BRIDGE

PHAITHUN THANYA

Translated by S. Surang

"WHAT a beautiful morning!" the bull keeper felt as he left his sleeping shed with a young bull before dawn. He coaxed the bull to run and walk alternately for almost ten kilometers. He liked to watch the young bull trot, its taut muscles undulating up and down, a sign of strength and unflagging determination similar to a boxer ready to pummel his fist into his opponent's face and defeat him in the bloody ring, as swiftly as a sparrow taking a drink of water. Running early morning was what he enjoyed doing. Since it was also his duty, he hardly ever missed it.

Every morning he would run with this bull. It was a serious exercise for the bull. The stake of almost three hundred thousand baht attached to its horns in this fight was high enough to persuade his master to think nothing of the cost of the best care. The man was, in fact, only a bull keeper. He had never earned anything more than a daily wage of thirty baht. At most, he would enjoy a delicious feast at his master's table to celebrate the victory, but only when the bull under his care actually won the fight.

The bull keeper strode on. He no longer prodded the bull to run as it had already had enough exercise for the morning, but he had to take it to walk around the sandy beach once more. This walk strengthened the bull's joints. Not only would the bull become stronger but he himself also. Now he could easily run more than twenty or thirty kilometers nonstop. Whenever it was market day, he would take the bull to parade there to accustom it to the big crowd. At the time of the fight, it would not be startled or scared. Bulls that found themselves in strange surroundings tend to be easily alarmed and run away from their opponents when they hear the shouts from people around the arena. Therefore, taking the bull to the market was another exercise that the bull keeper had to perform almost every morning. He himself preferred doing this to running a long distance. How proud and content he felt at the gaze from the crowd that watched him and the young bull walk by. At that moment he felt as if he were the real owner of this young red bull.

The morning sun radiated its warmth. The bull keeper ambled leisurely behind, allowing the spirited bull to saunter in front. He would take the lead again when they came near the bridge.

The sandy beach where the bull keeper would take the bull was on the other side of the river. He had to lead the bull across a narrow bridge which was wide enough for just one bull to pass. In fact no bull keeper would normally lead a bull across this bridge as it was no ordinary bridge but a "monkey bridge" made of big cables strung across and wooden planks for walking, with two strong wires on each side to hold on to. Whenever someone walked across, it would swing dangerously from one side to the other, to say nothing of when a bull crossed. A man not used to it would almost crawl across. But his fighting bull crossed it gracefully. It was a special feat, a difficult task that no other bull keeper could command a bull to perform, he thought.

The bull keeper had to walk backward across the bridge. It began to sway when the man and the bull stepped on it. He was a little surprised when the bridge lurched more than usual. At the same time his bull snorted and raised its ears as if it had seen an opponent. At that moment he heard another bull's snort from behind.

The bull keeper turned around suspiciously. He was taken by

surprise when he saw someone else leading a bull across this narrow bridge. It was also a fighting bull.

The two people faced each other in the middle of the bridge. There was a bull lead in each of their hands. The two bulls began to challenge each other. What a terrible coincidence.

The bridge swayed heavily when the two bulls approached each other. Each tried to push past through its owner. Both men and bulls were only six to seven meters apart.

The first bull keeper was greatly annoyed. He had never imagined anybody would dare to challenge him. It seemed as if he had been insulted and he could not take it lightly.

"Get your bull out of my way," he shouted angrily while using his hand to stop his bull from moving forward.

"Take yours away!" answered the second bull keeper, his face showing no trace of fear. His bull was milky white, its horns curved with ends sharp as thorns.

"You move back," said the keeper of the red bull, "We were on the bridge first. You came afterwards, so you get off first."

"Who said I came after you? You were walking backwards, how could you see?" the white bull keeper retorted and at the same time shouted to stop his bull's movement. In any case he could not back up, his bull was still very excited. It was not accustomed to this type of bridge but the bull keeper needed to get to the opposite bank where he had an appointment to show his bull to the village headman.

"Hey! Why don't you just move back?" the red bull keeper tried to keep his voice calm.

"I told you to move back. What are you on about?" The white bull keeper shouted back. His bull was more agitated than before.

The two men could not settle their argument. The red bull and the white bull were in full view of each other. They both tried to push past their keepers to the fore. They made more threatening noises. Both bulls' eyes shone menacingly green.

The bridge rolled noisily. Still neither bull keeper made a move. The noises made by the two young bulls were loud and fearless.

"Quickly, move quickly. Don't you see that the bulls are going to gore each other," the red bull keeper yelled at the top of his voice. He could no longer control his wrath.

"All you can do is shout out orders. If you are afraid to die, move back. I can't." The opponent became extremely angry. His breath quickened to the same pace as his bull.

"I'm not ordering, but isn't it right that you should move back first? You saw me walking backward. Why didn't you warn me first? You wanted to provoke me, didn't you?" The red bull keeper shouted back in the same tone. He seemed to be getting angrier.

"Don't cause trouble. I didn't mean to provoke you. You didn't watch where you were going and now are blaming others." The white bull keeper pointed his finger at his accuser and moved one step towards him. The young restless bull behind him moved up quickly.

"Whether you intended it or not, you provoked me." The red bull keeper refused to yield. "I bring my bull this way every day with no trouble. Only today has someone dared to copy me. You can't measure up to me."

"Hey! You've gone too far, much too far. You say I'm copying you. Any bull can cross this bridge. You think yours is so clever. Don't have such a big head. Your father doesn't own the bridge. Why can't I cross it?"

"How dare you mention my father! I can't take it any more. Although my father doesn't own this bridge, your mother didn't build it either." The red bull keeper trembled with anger, his finger pointing at the face of his antagonist.

Both bulls were more agitated, they faced off each other ferociously. Their keepers had to restrain them with full force. The bridge swayed more and more, the bridge cables groaned loudly. The green water below whirled slowly, ready to swallow up each body that fell in.

Both men looked fiercely at each other without yielding. The young red bull was restless. It resolutely tried to push past its keeper's body. So did the white bull. It pushed its keeper forward until he had to hit it. The bridge reeled as if it would turn upside down. Both men and bulls began to show their fear.

"Do you want all of us to die? Move back now, quickly. Can't you hear? We'll all die if you don't listen." The white bull keeper shouted again. His anger seemed to subside. He used one hand to hold tight onto the wire railing. The red bull keeper acted almost in the same manner.

"How can I go? The bridge is so narrow. The bull can't turn round. Do you want it to move backward? Let your bull try first. It's easier for them to run towards each other."

"Your bull can't turn round. Mine neither. What shall we do?" The white bull keeper's face turned pale. His bull was incessantly scratching at the wooden planks. It made the bridge sway more and more.

"Hey! Hey! What are you doing? Why are you baiting bulls in the middle of a bridge like this? Give me some room please." The shout came from behind the red bull keeper. At the same time, the sound of footsteps came closer and closer. A man was carrying a pole across his shoulders with one tub hanging on each side of the pole. The tubs were full of fresh rubber liquid which seemed so heavy that his waist leaned forward and his body swayed from side to side like that of a drunkard. The white rubber liquid spilt all over the bridge.

"Are you mad too? Why do you come on the bridge. Can't you see both men and bulls are blocking the way?" The red bull keeper turned around and yelled in annoyance at the newcomer because the latter caused the bull to become apprehensive and almost push him off the bridge.

"I am carrying heavy loads, how can I stop? Look, my rubber has spilt all over. The boss will really be mad at me today." The rubber carrier complained with annoyance. His legs were still trembling.

The red bull keeper pushed back his bull but it refused to budge. It only moved forward towards the white bull. The bridge began to sway again, causing the rubber liquid to spill more.

"Please, don't let the bulls fight—my rubber has spilt all over, can't you see? Don't you have any work to do? Baiting bulls in the middle of a bridge! This is not an arena. It causes trouble for others, can't you see?" The rubber carrier tried to keep his balance but couldn't because the bridge was still swaying.

"You know you can't pass, why don't you move back? Move back, quick, hurry up. If the bridge breaks, we'll all be dead, believe me." The red bull keeper was extremely annoyed. He left his former opponent for a moment and turned around to stare fiercely at the rubber carrier instead.

"Anyone can walk this way," retorted the rubber liquid carrier. "I come here every morning. I have never met such crazy men. How unlucky!" He continned to mutter but refused to turn back because he was afraid of spilling more rubber. If he lost all the rubber in both tubs, it would mean the loss of a whole day's wage. What a shame that would be.

Before the red bull keeper could answer back, the white bull keeper screamed loudly when another person stepped on the foot of the bridge in front of him. The agitated manner of the newcomer frightened his bull.

"Hey Ma'am! What are you coming on for? Can't you see that both men and bulls are blocking it? Hey! Stop. Stop right there. The bulls are frightened."

"Please make way. I'm going to the market. My child is dying. I'm going to buy some medicine. Move quickly please." The middle aged woman who had just stepped on the bridge seemed not to hear any warning. She did not see anything obstructing her. She only wished to move forward.

"You can't go, you can't go. Are you deaf?" The white bull keeper yelled at her at the top of his voice. He looked both angry and upset.

"Take away your bulls. Take them away, you bums. My child is dying. Let me pass to buy some medicine." She yelled loudly and quickly gripped the bridge railing precariously. "Why are you provoking me? Don't rock the bridge. Don't rock it. Hey! Don't!" She screamed hysterically.

"Hey! Woman! Don't struggle so hard. My rubber has spilt all over. Can't you see? Oh! I'm going crazy. Why must this happen to me?" the rubber carrier shouted from the other end of the bridge. It seemed he could not bear it any longer.

"Why don't you turn back? What are you complaining for? You are just like that woman. All she can do is scream. See? My bull is frightened. Soon we'll all fall into the water." The red bull keeper bawled at the man also.

The middle-aged woman trembled with the sway of the bridge. Her face showed her terror. She began to weep like a lunatic.

"Ma'am! You had better turn back. The bull is blocking everything. Don't you see? I tell you, you can't go. Why don't you believe me? A lot of people weigh down the bridge. Don't you see?" the white bull keeper reasoned with her again. His angry manner subsided when he saw how afraid the woman was. The two bulls were still breathing hard, ready to jump at each other as if they were in the arena.

The sun had risen quite high. The people on the bridge could not settle their argument. The two bulls were facing off to each other with every intent to fight. The bridge rocked to the bulls' struggling movements. The iron cables groaned alarmingly.

Two more people were stepping on the bridge, one on the side of the red bull keeper with his bicycle. On the white bull keeper's side was a monk returning from receiving alms. Both men came towards the middle of the bridge out of curiosity. The additional weight immediately made the bridge sink lower.

"What's the matter? What happened?" The man with the bicycle asked as he approached the rubber carrier who was standing perplexed.

"Are you crazy? Why do you bring the bicycle? Can't you see that the bridge is blocked?" The rubber carrier with empty tubs yelled at him.

"I can see quite clearly. But I wanted to know what the matter is, so I went up to find out," the man with the bicycle answered with a calm voice, as unemotional as his facial expression.

"Then why must you bring the bicycle? You could have left it at the foot of the bridge."

"How can I leave it there? A new bicycle like this! Some thief will have it."

"What a pain! What are you arguing for? You're all mad, the lot of you!" The red bull keeper yelled impatiently.

"Now. What's the matter? Do tell me. Why are you baiting bulls in the middle of a bridge like this? That's no fun," the middle-aged monk said when he reached the middle of the bridge.

"It's his fault." The white bull keeper pointed at his antagonist. "He led the bull up the bridge without looking."

"You're the one who's wrong. I was walking backwards. I couldn't possibly see that another man was on the bridge," unyielding, the red bull keeper retorted immediately.

"You yourself are totally wrong. And when others came, you accused them too."

"It's a lie." The white bull keeper jerked his hand angrily in front of him. The noisy argument frightened both bulls even more. They turned right and left and shifted about until the bridge creaked loudly. The red bull was startled when its heavy step broke a wooden plank.

"Help! The bridge is breaking up! Help!" The middle-aged woman was yelling, closing her eyes tight and trembling like a helpless chick.

On both sides of the bridge, more and more people were gathering. Those who wanted to cross the bridge shouted abuse. The people on the bridge were too agitated to know what to do.

The middle aged monk held his bowl tight in his hands. The drum signal sounding from the temple on the opposite bank made him anxious.

"Now. Now. Don't argue. All of you are wrong. You two have caused trouble for all of us. Those who want to cross the bridge cannot, can they? Now we had better find a solution before the bridge breaks up and we all die." The monk mediated and called out for the others to move back from the bridge. The bull keepers would move later.

Soon there were only the two bull keepers left on the narrow bridge. Yet they could not succeed in forcing their bulls back.

The shouts of the people on the banks was pressing them to move. The exclamations of abuse and annoyance frightened both bulls so much that they could not be constrained. They pushed their keepers back down until the pair crashed into each other in the middle of the bridge. Both bulls could see each other clearly once more. They made more heavy threatening noises against each other. The sharp ends of the horns were flashing close to the keepers' faces. The bridge swayed as if some unseen hand were rocking it. Both bulls were scratching their hoofs towards each other in a crazed manner. Their keepers could not use their hands to push them back even one step. The people on the banks shouted louder. Some urged the two bulls to fight out of spite.

Perspiration flooded the pale faces of the two bull keepers. Now neither was thinking of his own dignity or self-esteem. The backs of both men pressed against each other until they became almost one flesh. The four hands that were pushing the bulls' noses weakened more and more. The heavy roars and the hot breaths of both bulls were like the signals from the messenger of Yama, the god of death—then suddenly the bulls sprang into each other.

The cry of pain was heard simultaneously. The people on the banks put their hands over their eyes to avoid the horrible sight. The crack of the bulls' horns crashing against one another was as loud as thunder. The bridge swayed and tilted. The bodies of the two men collapsed between the sharp horns. Suddenly one of the bridge cables snapped. The bridge tilted and hit the water surface. Both men and bulls fell into the whirlpool.

The screams from the people on the banks lasted long. Then everything sank beneath the whirlpool. A few wooden planks floated around amidst the glittering water bubbles.

THE PROPHECY

PHAITHUN THANYA

Translated by Duangtip Surintatip

I
T had been there for a very long time . . . so long that nobody
knew from when it dated. Even those ancient village elders
who had long since died used to say that it was there as far
back as they could remember. Today its widespread branches and
deep roots sprawled over a wide area. It could be said that on as
much as a quarter of the village land, one was bound to unearth
roots wherever one dug. Its gnarled roots that emerged above the
ground, the tangled mass of its hanging roots, all pointed to the
fact that this banyan tree was the single oldest and most ancient
living thing in the village.

So many tales and wondrous legends about this great banyan
tree were imparted orally from grandparents to grandchildren for
numerous generations. As time passed, these tales became even
more fantastic. These were the elements that added immeasurably
to the myth of the great banyan until it daunted any who saw it
and inspired awe in those who had only heard the yarns. The spirit
house, remains of garlands and offerings, and traces of thick layers
of old and new silk sashes that bound the tree trunk were like a
sacred wall that sheltered it from defilement and disrespect. No
one ever asked why there should be these decorations around the
great banyan. Not a word was ever uttered by the elders to

encourage this seemingly vile act. These were just the teachings that must be believed in and followed.

2

IT had been there for a very long time . . . and could have continued to be there for a long time, had its powerful sprouting roots not disrupted the large ordination hall nearby. The million-baht ordination hall that had been the pride and joy of the monastery was now completely eclipsed by the branches and stems of the giant banyan, as if it would not allow anything to grow and compete with it for greatness. But this was not as bad as the invasion of its roots into the foundation of the ordination hall, causing a multitude of cracks to appear on the floor. As days went by, the cracks expanded so alarmingly that it was feared that the ordination hall's collapse was imminent.

This was the most aggravating problem. It presented a challenge to the ability of everyone responsible for the hall. It seemed that the abbot who looked after the temple in particular shouldered the heaviest burden of all.

"Which would you choose—the ordination hall or the great banyan?" The abbot posed the question to the temple council, expecting its members to provide an answer.

"Couldn't you think of anything else?" asked Pluang, one of the monastery committee members, thoughtfully.

"Could there be any other way? . . . You probably remember not so long ago how we tried to dig a ditch between the banyan and the hall to cut off its roots and stop them from growing under the hall. But the result was plain for all to see. The floor cracked more than ever before." The middle-aged scholar monk concluded his sentence with a long drawn-out sign. His words caused a momentary silence at the meeting.

The reddish orange glow of the large candle in front of the Buddha statue lit up the faces of all present. The candlelight picked out ever so clearly the frown on each face. Every mute body in the candlelight looked as sullen as each one of the stone statues in the deserted pavilion.

"Are we supposed to fell the banyan?" riposted Pluang anxiously.

"I don't think we have a better choice . . . We must keep the hall because we went through a lot of trouble to build it. As for that banyan . . ." The learned monk began to mumble.

"That banyan . . . I am aware that it is respected by everyone in the village. But all things considered, it has to be felled. We really have no choice. Whatever happens afterwards, I'll be responsible for . . ."

A murmur rippled around the circle once the monk had ended his speech. It was not an issue to be opined or decided on that easily. Nobody had ever dared to be so disrespectful to the great banyan. But this time, the idea came from the learned monk whom the villagers revered. Faced with his idea, others began to hesitate.

"What do you think? I mean everyone of you . . . Speak your mind!" insisted the monk who had noticed the councill members' reluctance to speak.

"It's up to you if you think it's all right. We don't see any way out either. If anything untoward happens, we shall not allow you to be blamed alone. Each and everyone of us is willing to share the responsibility," Wan, the most senior member of them all, declared firmly. The rest followed suit.

"Then let's get started. We should try out whatever we think right. We can't afford to delay the matter any longer," said the abbot, closing that evening's meeting.

3

LIKE a raging wild fire in the dry months, the account of that evening's meeting spread fast from mouth to mouth. Before the day's end, the villagers were making a meal of it. This was no ordinary run-of-the-mill story. It turned out to be an alarming piece of news that shook almost every villager to the core of their being. It was the worst news that ever hit this tiny village.

"Everybody is doomed. You'll see . . . " The village shaman, Plung, growled angrily at a large crowd. "They will be ruined utterly . . . anyone whoever dare to think ill of the sacred banyan tree will inevitably suffer the consequences. Which devil, I wonder, misled the abbot to this extent?" exclaimed the old man whose eyes glowered frighteningly.

"It was the right idea, old man. The abbot is doing the right thing. You mustn't forget that the ordination hall is worth millions. Who else but the abbot could have built it? You'd better think it over." Pluang could not help protesting. At least he was taking the same stance as the abbot.

"Pluang! You're just a kid. Are you trying to teach mantra to a *rishi*? Don't you see that the ordination hall can be bought? If you have money, you can make it look like a palace. But the venerable banyan . . . Where can you buy the venerable sacred banyan? You lot are morons . . . the bunch of you." The old man worked himself into a frenzy. He was not going to stop there.

"You people don't know any better. You don't know anything about the order of things. You should know that the venerable banyan has been the abode of spirits and angels for many many years. In every hollow and on every hold of each tree are deposited the bones of our ancestors. Our grandparents and their grand-parents buried the bones of the dead there. Anybody who thinks of destroying the sacred banyan is challenging the spirits and angels themselves. They shall die a horrible death . . . a horrible death . . . remember my words, remember! Ha! Ha!" The old shaman exploded in his rage. His declaration terrified all those who heard him. Almost every pair of eyes were focused on the temple councillors with hatred and mistrust. But most of them adhered to their original opinion. The elderly Wan in particular was never moved by criticism and prophecy.

"We are like someone riding on a tiger's back. We can't jump off its back and it's up to our fate whether we should live or die. Keep your spirits up. No matter what, the abbot is on our side." Wan firmly cheered up his friends.

Criticism on the subject of the giant banyan tree intensified. Those who were opposed to the felling recounted ancient legends on its miraculous and awesome feats that frightened their listeners. Others elaborated on what they had heard and told even taller tales. Every legend there was on spirits and nymphs was revived and recounted endlessly as if the entire village were prevailed over by the host of ghosts and spirits.

One evening, the noisy rumors were quashed by the mighty hum of a large tractor that arrived at the village. The deep imprints left on the ground by its clumsy belts intimidated all those who had seen them. The sharp edge of its giant white blades, capable of destroying everything in the path, was not unlike the sharp fang of an evil demon on its way to combat the great banyan. Each revving of its engine carried away the villagers' morale with its enraged sound wave. The awesome battle was about to start.

Because of the huge payment proposed by the temple council, the caterpillar tractor was brought all the way here. It moved boldly until it came to a stop a few meters away from the giant banyan. The gleaming white blades were lifted mid-air while it growled intermittently. Its posture was not unlike that of a proud bull, furiously stamping the ground to intimidate its foe.

The betting started. Every pair of eyes was wide open, unblinking. Every heart pounded to cope with each moment of excitement. The giant tractor howled once more its last, before turning on its heels and fleeing ignominiously from the arena. All the speculation unexpectedly came to an abrupt end.

"The driver was afraid that the spirit would possess him."

That was basically why he surrendered. As a result, the fantastic legends and miraculous powers of the giant banyan once more resonantly filled the entire village. This time, their noise was many times louder than before.

4

"ARE you really going to do it, Fua?" asked Fen incredulously.

"Would I joke about something like this?" retorted Fua before tipping his glass and making the clear liquid disappear into his throat. He then went on, "Are you in? We'll split the money fifty-fifty. You'll have booze money for a month at least. It's a cinch." Fua tried to extract an answer from his friend with a pointed stare.

"Are you out of your mind, Fua? This is no joke. Even a tractor had to run away. You and I are mere mortals. Do we stand a chance? Something evil will befall us before we can start. I'm really scared."

"Nonsense! Young people like us aren't supposed to be afraid of ghosts. Aren't you short of money? It's a cool three thousand! We'll get one thousand five each. You can use the money to ask for the hand of your girlfriend, Lamduan. Isn't your father-in-law pressing you? Just think about it—do you want Lamduan or not?"

Fen thought hard . . . It was true. He wanted so very badly to marry Lamduan whom he had courted for years. But he hadn't come up with any money to date. Lamduan's father brought up the subject at each meeting. The young policeman who owned that fabulous motorcycle paid her frequent visits. He couldn't afford to delay the marriage any longer. Nevertheless, the words of shaman Plang were implanted in both his ears. He didn't know what to do.

"I'm still scared." said Fen noncommittally. I've heard that they appeared in old Plang's dream last night. I mean the banyan ghosts . . . the whole bunch of them, from the very young to the very old. They came howling and pleading with him not to destroy their homes. People said that they spent the whole night crying. The one who was their leader threatened that if any disbeliever went and did something to the banyan tree, he would break their necks. Each time old Plang has such a dream, he is proved right. That's why I'm scared like I told you." Fen used the latest news as pretext while grimacing.

"Rubbish! Old Plang and his ghosts. When anything happens, he threatens you with ghosts. This banyan ghosts business, I've seen and heard the stories until I'm sick and tired of all of them. These stories of ghosts inhabiting big trees are all lies. If they were true, how come there are no big hopeas left in the forest. They have all been felled until there was none left. And nothing happened to the guys who felled them either. If anything, they seemed to prosper. Come on—are you in or not? I want to know right now." Fua stepped up the pressure.

"O.K." whispered Fen, his only thought was for the face of his beloved Lamduan.

5

IT had been there for a very long time . . . Every part that made up its gigantic trunk was itself huge. The sturdy trunk was wider than seven men surrounding it, arm to arm. It stood tall and solid like a mountain. Its trailing roots were entangled just like the long beard of a strange hermit. Each branch that grew out and spread into mid-air was thick and formidable. Every gust of wind howled through the branches like an evil spirit. Every part of the giant banyan tree was imbued with a mighty power that threatened one to the very bone.

Both of Fen's legs trembled. His heart pounded while his whole body was racked with raging hot and cold sensations. As soon as he entered the dark, enveloping shade of the great banyan, Fen felt as though it contracted his body into the size of a grain of sand. He looked up and stared at the tree. His hand that gripped the axe handle felt as cold and clammy as a snail. He could taste a musty emanating from the folds of the boles. He turned to take a look at his partner and found him humming a tune as if unperturbed.

"Hack at all of its branches. Tie up the branches near the roof with a rope before chopping them. Watch out for your hands and feet. Once all the branches are down, we can pour a stump-killing solution over it. I guarantee that the tree will decompose and turn into loose soil in two months." A member of the monastery board explained what to do nearby but it seemed to Fen like a whisper from a faraway place.

"How are you doing?" shouted Fua good-humoredly while taking a swipe at the hanging roots with his big knife. "We've got to get rid of all these dangling roots before cutting off the top branches. In ten days' time, there'll be nothing left except a stump. That is if our necks haven't been broken like you said." Fua spoke half jokingly but his words sent a shudder through Fen's heart.

The sacred banyan of the village was being challenged by two small humans. One had the reckless courage of youth and balked at nothing. Any opening that could bring in some money to buy booze with was a fair deal to him. The other human was more sensitive and less cocksure than his mate despite being of the same age. But his yearning heart somehow made him forget his misgivings.

Only three days went by. The ancient, ramified branches of the shady giant banyan tree were untidily lopped off by the hands of the two tiny young men, amidst the fear and trepidation felt by nearly half of the population of the entire village. Despite the curses and doomsday prophecies, the two youngsters' defiant task progressed relentlessly. The sixth, seventh, and eighth days came and went. Today was already the ninth and nothing could possibly halt the blades of the machetes in the hands of Fen and Fua. The ever-watchful temple councillors were able to smile expansively, showing not a trace of yesterday's apprehension.

The noon sun erupted in an angry burst of light when a branch of the banyan was pulled apart and came crashing down on the other side. The sun that in former days had found no way to pierce through the dense foliage was given its first chance. Under the scorching sun Fen and Fua stood back to back. Their muscular backs were soaked in sweat and reflected the sunlight like a polished surface. While Fua was cutting some intertwining twigs above a bole of the banyan, the blade of his machete struck hard against a solid object that lay buried underneath a small mound. The loud noise caused Fen to turn at once and ask hurriedly, "What is it, Fua?"

"I don't know. It felt like a rock or a chunk of solid iron," answered Fua in a croaking voice while digging at the spot with his bare hands. After a short while, Fua's hand touched a cold, hard object.

His heart pounding, Fua carefully prized it out with one hand. Fen stepped in to give a helping hand. In one breath, the two men's hearts almost stopped beating.

"An urn . . . for bones," hollered Fua excitedly

"It's a gold urn . . . real gold, Fua," Fen gibbered. Despite being coated in a film of rust and dirty mud, the urn glittered brightly.

The two exchanged a meaningful look. Their eyes barely concealed a welling sense of joy. Fua was already beside himself.

"Hide it, Fua. Bury it for now. People down there are watching us." Fen was the first to regain his composure.

"We'll come back for it tonight," whispered Fua in a trembling voice. Both understood one another. Fua buried the urn at the original spot, while Fen shouted to the men down below that Fua's machete had hit a rock.

The two men resumed their work. Their minds drumming up wild thoughts. Each was dreaming and banking on the chance discovery in the bole of the bayan.

"Tonight, let's meet at midnight." Fua whispered a determined promise before they left each other and headed for home as dusk fell.

6

THE crowd that formed a circle gathered more people quickly. By the time the rising sun emerged above the east woods, the area underneath the banyan cluttered up with withering branches and twigs, the circle had become a congregation of the whole village.

The body that lay on its back amidst the banyan twigs appeared to all staring eyes to have breathed its last at least five to six hours ago. Its condition gave an inkling of a fierce struggle before death. Both eyeballs showed their whites and bulged out of their sockets. A blue tongue was stuffed tightly in its mouth, with only its tip sticking out. Traces of clotted blood oozed out of both cheeks. The neck was ringed with blue bruises as if it had been kneaded or violently strangled. When someone poked at the head with a branch, he managed to turn it round in a full circle. But most astonishingly, the body was completely surrounded by scattered pieces of rotten bones.

"Fua! Poor Fua! You shouldn't have come to this," interjected someone sadly. The encircling crowd murmured.

"Didn't I say so? . . . Wasn't I right when I foresaw this? All of us who are gathered here, take it all in with your own eyes. What I prophesied has turned out to be true, hasn't it? I warned you but nobody believed me. You took me for an old fool of a shaman. Now you can plainly see that Fua's neck was broken. Who broke his neck? Why did he have to come and die here? Was it not because of the holy banyan tree? This is what happens to those who insult holy beings. Remember this as a lesson. Will there be anyone else who doesn't believe me? Ha! Ha!" Plang the shaman shouted smugly to the face of the abbot, the temple councillors, and every villager present. The old shaman's declaration seemed like a fitting conclusion, a confirmation and an end to the lengthy speculations. The result had been death.

The abbot looked up from the corpse in front of him. His face expressionless, he glanced around the crowding circle. Then in a calm and collected voice that rang with authority, he said.

"Now, listen everyone . . . Please hear me out. Since Fua is dead whether because the spirit broke his neck as old Plang said, or of whatever cause, we'll still have to find that out. Right now I want you to take heart. Death is inevitable. Everyone must come to it. Fua has died and paid for his karma. I will take care of his body. You don't have to worry about it. The temple councillors and I will do whatever is necessary. But I beg you to use your judgment before believing in anything for sure. As for Fen . . . ," The abbot hesitated a moment before turning towards Fen. His piercing and frigid stare forced the ashen-faced Fen nearby to look the other way.

"Fen will have to finish the work now that there's only one branch left. Whatever will be, will be. You just have to finish it off, understand?" The middle-aged monk ended his speech, then with a wave of his hand, quietly asked for a way out of the ring.

Fen heaved a huge sigh before the watching crowd erupted in yet another murmur.

MID-ROAD FAMILY

SILA KHOMCHAI

Translated by Chancham Bunnag

M Y wife is marvelously well-organized. She thinks of everything. When I tell her I have an important appointment at three o'clock in the afternoon (to be with the boss when he meets a big client at a riverside hotel in Khlongsan[1] area), she says we need to leave the house at nine o'clock as she herself has to be somewhere in the vicinity of Saphan Khwai[2] before noon. This is just right to get us to both places in time, thanks to her planning.

More thanks are called for. Look at the back seat of our car. She's provided us with a basket of fast food, an icebox full of bottled drinks, all manner of cakes and tidbits, green tamarind, star gooseberry, a salt shaker, a plastic bag for trash, a spittoon (or chamber pot). There is even another set of clothes hanging from the grip above the mirror. It looks as though we're going on a picnic.

Theoretically we belong to the middle class. You can deduce that from the location of our house, which is in the northern residential suburbs of Bangkok between Lum Luk Ka and Bang Khen. To get into town from our place, you drive past a number

1. area on the west bank of the Chao Phraya River opposite to Bangkok
2. well-known area near central Bangkok

of housing projects, one after another after another and still more, then turn to Kilometer 25 on Phahonyothin Road, get on Viphavadi Rangsit Highway at the *Chetchuakhot* Bridge[3] and head for Bangkok. This is the easy way.

If we were of the very poor classes, we might be squatting somewhere in a slum in the center of town. The upper-class people also live around that area, in their condominiums where they can watch the golden sunset reflected in the rippling river.

More important than that is the golden dream forever glittering before them.

The upper-class goal is plain to see, but how to get there—that's the problem. So we work like mad whilst devising all sorts of schemes. Our great hope and plan is to have our own business and this, no doubt about it, is an almost daily obsession. Meanwhile, we've achieved what it is in our capacity to achieve: our own house and car.

What is the reason for having a car? That it is in order to upgrade one's status I will not deny. But more important is the fact that one's body has started to protest that it can no longer suffer being squashed and squelched and crushed in the bus for three to four hours at a stretch, while it tries to hang on to the strap as the bus creeps another inch on the scorched surface or gets stuck in a traffic snarl and stands absolutely still. When you have a car you can at least sink into the air-conditioned coolness and listen to your favorite songs. This is an infinitely better fate, you must admit.

Strange to think about it. I am 38 years old. I come home about eleven o'clock at night totally exhausted—even the simple act of getting into bed requires a supreme effort; and this is me, who used to play half (or mid-field as it is now called) in our school football team and was hailed a human dynamo. Now it feels as though every sinew in my body has gone slack, lost its bounce, outlived its span of usefulness.

3. "Seven Generations" Bridge, so named after the length of time taken to complete construction.

Perhaps it is because of overwork. But according to a radio piece I heard between melodies, our body systems have been eroded by the polluted air and its poisonous properties. Of course, the stress-and-strain in our lifstyle also shares the responsibility for sapping our strength.

A car is a necessity, a refuge. You spend as much time in it as in the house and the office. And when your wife has put things in it to make it as comfortable and convenient as possible it does become a veritable home, a real mobile office.

Thus I have ceased to feel frustrated in Bangkok traffic jams. It does not matter how many millions of cars are choking up the roads, it's normal to camp overnight behind the wheel. Life in the car brings the family closer. I really like that. Sometimes we eat lunch together when stuck on the expressway. It's very cosy. It's amusing. When the car has remained stationary for an hour or so, we may even grow quite playful.

"Close your eyes," my wife commands me.

I don't get it and ask "Why?"

"Just do it." She says, then brings the spittoon from the back seat, puts it on the floor, hitches up her skirt and slides down under the steering wheel. I place a hand on my eyes and peep at her flesh (not new to me) through spread fingers. Such a moment on the road arouses my senses with excitement.

"You're cheating." She makes mock-angry eyes at me after finishing what she has to do, and gives me a few poundings with her fist to cover up her sense of bashfulness.

We married at a mature age, as advised by the Ministry of Public Health, and furthermore, we strictly adhered to the slogan about waiting for when we're good and ready before starting a family. We are provincial folks who had to struggle to make it to the big city and build our fortune. So when we finally reach the state of near-readiness for parenthood I am thirty-eight and my wife thirty-five and, physically speaking, not in very good shape for the task. It's not so easy when you come home exhausted at eleven o'clock and climb wearily into bed after midnight. Some desire is there but the chemistry is weak, and since we seldom do it the chance of starting a family must be slim.

One day I had woken up feeling especially bright and cheerful
—must have had a good sleep for a change. Yes, cheerfully I woke
up, let the sunshine caress me, breathed in the fresh air, executed
some samba steps by way of exercise, bathed and shampooed and
drank a glass of milk and ate two soft-boiled eggs. And began to
feel a little like the old mid-field hero I used to be.

There was a traffic obstacle on Viphavadi Rangsit Road,
announced my favourite D. J. on the radio. And a ten-wheel truck
had just crashed into a lamp post in front of the Thai Airways
International head office. The road was being cleared . . .

I was feeling hale and hearty.

In the car to the left two teenagers, or may be they were in their
early twenties, were having fun with each other. The boy rumpled
the girl's hair. She pinched him. He put his arm round her
shoulder and drew her close to him. She poked her elbow in his
ribs and . . .

I came alive as though I were in that field of action myself. I
turned to eye my wife and found her more attractive than usual.
My eyes left her face and travelled to her swelling bosom, then to
her thighs and knees. Her very short skirt was pulled up
dangerously high to facilitate driving.

"You have such beautiful legs," I told her. My voice shook, my
heart beating fast.

"Don't be crazy," she said, though not seriously. She looked up
from her well-tended nails, lifting her face to reveal the smooth
complexion and contour of her neck.

I swallowed hard, looked away, trying to calm the troubling
tingling inside me. But the image continued to disturb me and the
imagination refused to be controlled. The animal had been stirred,
especially the higher animal seeking new untried pleasures with an
appetite run wild.

My hands grew clammy as I glanced round at the other cars in
the stalled traffic. They all had tinted windows like ours. It was so
lovely and cool in ours. The piano concerto from the radio flowed
like water, quietly yet in turmoil. My trembling hands pulled the
anti-glare plastic sheets down over the tinted windows. Our private
world for that moment floated in sweetness and light.

This I know: we human beings have destroyed nature outside and within us and now we find ourselves trapped and stifled in city-living, in pollution, in strangling traffic; that all this has wreaked havoc with the rhythm and tempo of normal family activities; and that the natural flow of life's music keeps getting suddenly turned off, or disrupted, or thwarted from the very start.

Perhaps on account of the long deprivation, plus that maternal yearning for a baby and some other reasons, "You're ruining my clothes" and the rest of her objections lost out to our more urgent demand to create and enjoy our mid-road nuptial home for its heavenly duration.

Togetherness has always been a feature of our married life: the crossword, the scrabble, and all the other games we have known. Now we knew them together again, and we were as we had been when we first fell in love. Reports from the radio stations told of the worsening Bangkok traffic: the whole of Sukhumvit, Phahonyothin, Ramkamhaeng, Rama IV. You name it. No movement anywhere.

As for me, it was as though I was in my own living room, lying on my favourite couch.

* * *

ONE of my plans concerns the car. I aim to get a bigger one, so as to allot more space to eating, playing, sleeping, relieving ourselves. And why not?

These days I pick up important contacts from neighboring cars stuck in the traffic. When cars don't move some of their passengers get out for a little walk and muscle-stretching. I do the same. We greet one another and chat about this and that: commiserate over the stock exchange, comment on politics, discuss economic conditions and business trends and sport events, and all.

Among my neighbors on the road: Khun Wichai, marketing director of a firm making sanitary towels; Khun Pratchaya, owner of a seafood cannery; Khun Phanu, manufacturer of a chemical solution for easy ironing. I can talk to all of them, for I work in advertising and have access to relevant data on consumers' values and preferences and such like. I must say I have acquired quite a few customers out of these cultivated-on-the-road relationships.

Naturally, a hard worker like me is much appreciated by the boss. He considers me his right-hand man. Our appointment today is with the owner of a brand new soft drink, 'Sato-can'. We are to help him promote his product from the word go, from inventing a brand name that's catchy to the ear, easy on the eye and lilting on the lips, to the mapping out of a long-term, comprehensive, minutely detailed campaign strategy. The annual 10-million-baht budget should give us plenty of scope for media exposure, subtle image building, hard-sell follow-ups, and so on and so forth. I will be there with the boss to help him present our brilliant proposals to the client in the most effectively persuasive manner.

* * *

IT is only a quarter past eleven. The appointment is at three o'clock. I have time to think about work, and to dream about that new car which would be more commodious, more accommodating. I can assure myself it is not an impossible dream.

Another stoppage is fast forming up—a long line of vehicles extends into the distance ahead of us . . . But this is exactly where on that memorable day the two of us built our nuptial home in the sun behind the anti-glare plastic sheets on the tinted windows . . .

I lie back and close my eyes. I try to think of the appointment to come, but my heart is racing.

It is as though the spell of passion still hovers over this portion of the road. What happened that day—the feeling that we were doing something improper, something to hide, to hurry over. Then there was the difficult maneuvering of bodies in limited space. It was all daring and exciting, like climbing over a wall to steal mangosteens from a temple when you were a child . . .

. . . Her pretty outfit was badly crumpled, and not solely due to my attack. For the hungry response had heated the car as if we had neglected to service the air-conditioning. Her hands gripped mine like a vice, then passed to my shoulder, hurting it with her nails.

I reach out to pull down the anti-glare sheets.

"No," she cries, then looks at me in the eye. "I don't know what's the matter with me. I feel awfully dizzy."

I sigh, turn away, pull myself together, reach for the food basket and take a sandwich as though the real hunger could be thus satisfied. My wife, who seems not at all well, chews a green tamarind and immediately perks up.

Feeling bored after the sandwich, I get out of the car and give a mirthless smile to fellow car-leavers some of whom are swinging their arms about, some bending and stretching their backs, some walking to and fro. The atmosphere resembles a housing complex where members have emerged from their respective residences to do their morning exercise on the communal ground. I feel they are my neighbors living in the same complex.

A middle-aged man wielding a spade is digging up a patch of earth on the island in the middle of the road. What a bizarre act on such a morning, but intriguing too.

So I go over to him and ask what he is doing.

"Planting a banana tree," he replies to the spade. It is only after finishing his job that he turns to me with a smile. "Banana leaves have ample length and width and can absorb much of the toxic elements in the atmosphere." He talks like an environmentalist. "I do this whenever there's a jam. Here, would you like to have a go. We'll be here quite sometime. The radio says there are two accidents involving seven or eight cars, one at the foot of the Lad Phrao Bridge, the other in front of the Mo Chit Station."

He passes me the spade and I take it. "All right," I say. "Pretty soon we'll have a banana grove here."

Actually, I am no stranger to this sort of work, having done it as a rural boy in my old province. The spade and the soil and the banana not only rescue me from boredom but also take me on a journey back to the long-forgotten days, for which I feel very grateful.

"If this island were filled with trees," he says, "it would be so nice, like driving through a plantation."

When we are through tending our garden and exchanging name cards, he asks me to have a cup of coffee in his car. I thank him but excuse myself because I have been away from the car long enough and should get back.

* * *

"I don't think I'm up to it. Will you do the driving, please."

Her face is ashen, covered with beads of sweat. She's holding the plastic bag close to her mouth.

"What's the matter?" I ask, surprised to see her in such a state.

"Dizzy, queasy, sick."

"Shall we go see a doctor?"

"Not now." She looks at me for an instant. "I missed my period the last two months. I think I'm pregnant."

I gasp, go cold like a log for a second or two before shouting hurray to myself—*Chaiyo! Chaiyo!* She vomits into the plastic bag. The noise and the smell bother me not at all. I merely want to leap out of the car and cry out:

"My wife is pregnant! Do you hear? She's pregnant! We did it on the road."

I take the wheel when the traffic moves once again, and I dream of the little one who will make our life complete, and of the new bigger car spacious enough to comfortably house father, mother, and baby, and all the multifarious items a family should have in order to carry out its various daily activities.

A bigger car is a necessity. We must have it as soon as possible if we wish to live happily for ever on the road.

"SAWDUST BRAIN"
AND THE WRAPPING PAPER

SILA KHOMCHAI

Translated by Duangtip Surintatip

T HE machine was working. It had its own rhythm, generating two or three different tones, repeating themselves all day long. It took only three or four short breaks per day. On the huge press bed two zinc-covered form rollers were moving horizontally and swiftly away from each other in opposite directions. White sheets fed in on one end were squeezed out on the other as magnificent colorful posters.

The one-story building was filled with the stale smells of printing ink, kerosene, new paper, and a host of other things indicating the nature of the activity. The humming noise of the machine was normal and did not get on anyone's nerves. Seated on a low stool, a boy aged thirteen or fourteen spread his legs around a neat pile of pristine, crispy thin sheets. His hands were busy folding one large sheet into sixteen sections, one for each page. A quick glance at the main door where three men were walking through spurred his hands on in a frantic circle-like movement. He did not attract their attention, and two of the men were his bosses.

"Could you hurry up with my order, boss? I've already told the delivery people that they should get them next week . . . " said one man, wearing a fading short-sleeved jersey neatly tucked inside his trousers' waist-band, one hand carrying a battered leather briefcase.

The other man was sporting a long-sleeved pink shirt, completely buttoned up, a necktie, dark trousers, and gleaming shoes.

"Uh-huh . . . Just be patient. We do have a lot of work on at the moment," the man groaned noncommittally.

"What's on the press bed?" asked the owner of the battered briefcase.

"Posters." The three approached the press bed.

"Why didn't you do mine first? When I sent in the order, you said you were free. I didn't see any of them."

"Come on . . . this is an urgent job. They've paid cash up front for the whole lot. There were a lot more of these poster jobs but I didn't dare take them on. I'm checking with my buddies to see which of them didn't pay last time so that I can blacklist them," the pink-shirted man said while stretching out his arm to reach one of the freshly printed sheets for a good look.

"Hey! This is the rich mine-owner from my hometown. Is he running in the election too?" The battered-briefcase owner craned his neck to get nearer, eyes fixed.

"How do you like it? He looks good. His face is well filled out. These royal decorations that pack his chest, don't know if they're genuine or fake!"

"Must be the real thing . . . The bastard is damn rich . . . When the field marshal was in power, he certainly filled his pockets. He offered to plant rubber trees for the field marshal free of charge in thousands of *rai*,[1] but asked in return for all the standing timber in the area. It was a virgin forest with good hard wood. The rubber trees were huge—the width of three to four men, arm-to-arm, and there were thousands of them. There was redwood, and other kinds of hardwood. The forest was razed until the ground was as bare as a monkey's bottom . . . " The owner of the battered briefcase spilled the words out in a torrent.

The third man was wearing only a vest, his pot-belly hardly contained in his shorts. He was not in the least interested in the conversation; instead, he watched the machine at work, the machine-minder twisting a knob here and there. The man looked

---

1. Thai land measurement equal to 1,600 square meters

around, watching a young man washing plates, a burly man pushing piles of sheets, a few workers smoking while waiting, a woman binding books by sewing in the middle while another woman trimmed edges. The fat man decided to stride towards the boy, and towered over him arms akimbo, pot-belly bulging, one corner of the mouth stretched while staring at the boy's hands at work.

"No! No! Not like that . . ." He cried out, almost yelling.

"Fold it first by half . . . left and then right . . . No! No!" his hands were flying this way and that. Finally, not fully satisfied, he bent over and snatched the sheet from the boy's hands.

"Can't you see these figures for the pages? When you fold the sheet, the pages must run from one to sixteen like this. Can't you count?" The man showed the boy how to do it. The boy followed the man's movement with uncomprehending eyes, his brain not responding. When he tried to fold the sheet like the man he still could not do it.

"No . . . pay attention . . . like this . . ." He stressed every word, totally fed up. The sheet in the boy's hands was turned over and over several times until crumpled.

"What's the matter with you? There is probably nothing but sawdust in your head. Take a look at this, they are all wrong. He picked up the boy's finished work and inspected it. The boy's face went pale, his lips trembling.

"What a waste! You've been here for nearly a week but don't seem to be able to do anything properly. What can we train this sawdust brain to do?" His eyes were harsh, his menacing voice grated. The boy shrank back, hunching up his shoulders.

"Go away! Don't fold any more. Let someone else do it. Go and wrap up those books. Bring that pile of fouled-up paper. What an idiot! Yesterday I asked him to buy fried rice noodles with soy sauce and I got stir-fried noodles with eggs instead," the fat man grumbled non-stop. The boy slunk slowly away, trying to hide from those heated sizzling words . . . Why isn't it as easy as planting corns in a field in the wilds of Loei province? You simply poke a small hole in the ground with a digger, throw in three or four seed corns, then use your foot to cover the hole with loose soil. You wait until the rain comes and wets the dark soil. The little pointed leaf that shoots up just above the soil surface is a lovely green."

"The guy amassed enough capital to run a mine. He was selling both illegal and legal ores. He got so rich, it's nobody's business," the battered-briefcase owner was holding forth at the other end of the room.

Is my head really filled with sawdust? The boy mused about this while holding in his arms the pile of paper. Teacher at school used to scoff at me, saying by the time he dragged me through to grade six, it was more difficult than dragging a branch by its top end. Mother is so heartless. She pushed me out as soon Uncle said he world take me to learn how to earn a living. The boy sorely missed his ground lizard hunting dog. Who would feed him now?

Anxiety and frustration filled his head. It made him feel even more confused. Perhaps the sawdust had grown in weight and was pressing against the inside of his head even more.

"Thirty copies a bundle. Arrange them in two rows and count before . . . No, not like that. Put the spines up fifteen to a row. Fold the length up and press it like this. Then take the other length like this . . ." The fat man showed him again how to wrap. His voice and overbearing manner pressured the boy's tiny body even more.

"Fold the bottom end into a triangle . . . like so, like so . . . Get rid of some of the sawdust in your head."

The boy slowed down now, following the movement studiously. He carefully laid down the rejected sheets that had been used in the try-out. Multi-colored sheets. Repeated try-outs resulted in foul, disgusting colors. Pictures were mixed up, one on top of another. Strips of colors laid across one another in a tangled formless mass. What a headache! Count the books and put them down. Fold the wrapping paper tightly.

"This man . . . does he stand a chance?" the pink-shirted boss asked the battered-briefcase owner at the other end.

"He'll win hands down . . . He wields power over two or three districts. He has so many henchmen they nearly tread on each other's toes. He's heavy-handed with donations too. Even the governor holds him in high regard."

" Ha . . . " The boss groaned and sighed.

The boy got on with his work. The fat man had moved away. His heart now relaxed from its relentless pounding. He kept glancing at each sheet. At this stage, the pictures and colors that piled dirtily on top of one another seemed partly to allay his fear and anxiety. The picture deep down in the layers was probably a field or patches of grass. There were some buffaloes and palm trees. Their color was greyish brown or murky green because the picture on top of it was a row of high-rise buildings. Many lines criss-crossed with bright electric lights. Other parts were too messy to make out.

The boy focused his eyes on the buffaloes. His mother spent her time with buffaloes and rice fields all year round and he missed her dreadfully. Wasn't her head filled with sawdust like his? . . .

Another sheet had a clear picture of a field. No buffaloes there. A nude lay twisted under a shady tree, showing off her pearly white skin. This looked like a centerfold from the kind of magazine that Uncle liked to hide underneath his pillow. It was clear because the superimposed print was in faded blue. It showed the portrait of a man, chest studded with medals, with letters in bold print on the very top. The boy read the message letter by letter, slowly, as if spelling out the words "VOTE FOR . . . " The nude woman was reclining right between his eyebrows.

"Gambling-dens . . . brothels . . . He got his hands in everything. From a common Chink . . . he's now a rich mine owner . . . the bastard . . . Look at the way he chose a nice picture for the poster. His real face is perforated like a laterite road." The battered-briefcase owner continued to discuss the man in the picture.

The books were now wrapped up tightly in square blocks. The boy piled the blocks up high. He had never done this work before in his life and it was a real torture to him.

The new rejected sheet looked like a poster advertising a Thai film. He remembered very well the star Soraphong standing with legs widespread and a gun in his hands. Who could the heroine be? He tried to search for her face, covered by the contour of a full head of well-greased, black hair of the man with the decorated chest under the letters "VOTE FOR . . . THE PARTY" that was just coming through. All he could see was a pair of shapely legs, difficult to tell whom they belonged to, the star Charuni or Sinchai, with thick wads of banknotes on the bridge of the man's nose and Soraphong's gun that seemed to have been aimed from the man's forehead.

The boy felt a surge of relief. His work was going smoothly. To see the film posters had made him happy. He thought of the many Thai movies he had seen. The hero was always a fighter, an honest decent man, self-sacrificing to the point of being admired by all. He himself had often dreamed of becoming . . .

"His rivals will fall on their face in droves." The pink-shirted man added.

"Yes . . . all Thais as well." The owner of the battered briefcase agreed.

The fat man took a look around as if to check whether everything about the operation was in order. He turned back to stare at the boy and the tension enveloped him again. The boy quickened his hands and counted the copies even more carefully. Anyway he was now much happier. To be able to look at these try-out sheets over and over again had revealed to him hidden stories. His mind was pulled out and lifted up and away from the drab and musty one-story building. They were like the only friends that he had, even though they were no ground lizard hunting dog —these sheets that the printer fed into the press to try out the pigments' consistency and their sharpness, and to absorb the kerosene left over from cleaning the press bed of the old colors.

"I really want to know, deep down inside, what's he after in volunteering for the post . . . " The boss murmured as if talking to himself at the other end.

At this end, the boy's hands trembled a little as he spread out another wrapping sheet. The drab and musty one-story building barred his way to the blue sky and the familiar dark green mountain ranges. He was submerged in the humming noise and anxiety. Despite being a little fearful, the boy could not suppress a smile. This time the picture was so sharp and clear that there was nothing left to make out. It was like an intentional experiment where everything fell in place. There was almost no blotted or blurred spot. It told a strange tale.

Was it possible that something like this could happen to an ordinary person? . . . He calmly took it all in. Suddenly the connection with himself hit him. And then his humor exploded. He burst into a fit of laughter.

The inside of his head, invisible though it was, contained nothing but sawdust. The man in the picture—his plight was even worse . . .

"You're crazy. What the hell are you laughing at, Sawdust Brain? What have you found, Sawdust?" The fat man had looked at the boy suspiciously for a moment and, able to stand it no longer, had shouted out the question. The boy could not stop the laugh and gave no reply. The fat man had to scoff at him again.

"His head . . . it . . . " The reply came in spurts, making no sense. His body swayed and shook in time with his emotion.

The noise managed to reach the other end, distracting the men. The briefcase owner turned to look at its source. The boy's uncontrollable gestures and hysterical laughter were contagious. It went on and on for quite some time. The briefcase owner then had an idea that there was something out of the ordinary. His curiosity pushed him nearer. When he saw the picture he joined the boy in roars of laughter.

"He's got worms in his head . . . worms . . ." He repeated while laughing at this incredible circumstance.

The picture embedded deep in the middle of the man's head underneath the bold print "VOTE FOR" looked like a nest of worms. They were creeping and crawling over one another until they made up a round ball. What was even funnier was that some worms were arching over the corner of the man's mouth, crawling out of his nostrils and ear-holes, making the whole thing resemble the picture of a corpse with a heavily decorated chest—a dead man whose eyes remained wide open and whose face brimmed over with perfect health.

MERE MOVEMENT

NAOWARAT PONGPAIBOON

Translated by Chancham Bunnag

A mere flutter of an eagle's wings
tempers the heat of the sun.
A mere trembling of a single leaf
announces the coming of the wind.

A mere glint in reflecting ripples
to proclaim clear water; no, not glass.
A mere little pain shining in the eyes
to declare the existence of the heart.

The clanking chains at the locked gate
make great the moaning of misery
while a pale light flickering yonder
whispers: "There's a way, There's a way."

The fist long-waiting, sweaty, heated,
strikes at last—what bliss!—strikes and falls,
heaves and falls again, each time knowing
what it is to taste of bliss.

The stricken fingers, feebly clinging, move
strong enough to impart strength
like the slim weed blades that sway
their honored heads above the rocky cracks.

An emptiness of four-zero years.
A stillness from four zero million.
Soil turned into sand, wood into stone.
Wholly still, unseeing, heedless.

As the bird heedless of heaven,
the fish unaware of water,
or the earthworm wrapped in earth
or the maggot blind to the filth.

Decay over the quiet bog does creep;
Yet out of the rot there arise
the first faint stirrings —the merest move
and a fine field of lotus awaits.

A promise astir, of nothing evil,
but of grace, and beauty, taking shape.
There amid the murky stillness,
the beginning is begun.

Listen to the temple drums.
Observe another Holy Day.
Hear the booming of the guns
mark the people's battle-cry.

THE WAY OF THE SNAIL

NAOWARAT PONGPAIBOON

Translated by Michael Wright

Through the tall weeds runs a path
Lonely and unvisited;
There the little snail paints his silver path,
A shining road

Waiting for the day
When the blazing sun
Will lash out in anger with its rays
And consume the weeds' domain.

Then the lovely silver,
Will be caught by the rays
And in a blaze like diamonds
Be consumed, the snail's track.

This piece was written during the "October uprising", 1973, which toppled the Thanom-Prapat government. The "weeds" mean illegal, despotic rule; the "little snail" stands for the many obscure folk who lost their lives on Bangkok's streets in those days.

And the little snail will offer up its flesh
To become a creator
From its own dissolution
As it has always been.

So there lies the way
Leading to the ideal.
As long as weeds rule
There will be hearts to struggle.

There's always pain in creation
Agony and stress
Like the lightning in the rain
Like gold in dull rock.

Come then, come bear it,
This suffering with friends
Don't hope that without it
Your life will shine.

The first steps that we take
Will paint a path
And there's much land untrod
Where we may go.

A BEGGAR'S CHANT

KHOMTHUAN KHANTHANU

Translated by Chancham Bunnag

My ten fingers down
　　　with my head on the ground
　　　at your passing feet
give me some coins please
pity me too weak to rise
pity me lost in misery
wife children sickly weary
starving on tears
give me an old rag
　　even that will do
　　　　even that will do

me a stray bird
come to town from Suphan
my accent's funny*
but don't spurn me
oh you who dress so pretty
keep this beggar alive

*Suphan, shortened from Suphan Buri, is a province in the central plains of Thailand and is known for its unique accent.

give half a cup of rice
half a hand of bananas
make merit for once
and win my thanks forever
     now and forever
          now and forever

lazy we were not
servile we were not
we tilled and ploughed
we farmed the land
and reaped the debts
the rich are big brothers
we owe money we the dogs
our tongues hang out
our bellies rumble
rice farmers begging rice from others
     can anyone understand
          can anyone understand

we beg we lose honor
become rubbish stricken despised
we beg we pant we pine
while the pain stabs our bellies
our children amoaning
asobbing agroaning
we look for coins, tears blind our eyes
we fall we die
     the beggars' caravan moving
from rice fields to streets
the dead are buried the living go hungry
every hair of the body cries aloud
          they know not of hunger

their wide world's all smiles
their heads are high their bellies bloated their feet frail

their children in money aplenty
their skins are very thick
they toil very hard
they plough and press and pluck
and spread all over town
        they mow you down who dare to rise
they tame you into pets
they take turns coming on top
they have fame and crave for more
they beg and threat and squeeze
they take and grab and rant and lust
they talk low think low and act low
my friends you very well know
    who they are
        who they are

A POET'S PLEDGE

ANGKARN KALAYANAPONG

Translated by Chamnongsri L. Rutnin

Who would dare trade skies and oceans?
Wondrous creation is this world of ours
These corporeal parts shall be laid
Betwixt earth and sky in the final hours.

We are not owners of clouds or air
Or the heavens or any element of earth
Man has made neither moon nor sun
Nor a single atom in a grain of sand.

Man cheats and kills to grab empires
Galvanized by greed, the breathing corpse
Spurns goodness and forgets its grave
Abdicating the dignity of the human soul.

Components and elements of this earth
Are worth all the celestial treasures
Forever cherish soil, sky and water
Make the world brighter than the heavens. Fields,

forests and impenetrable wilds
High mountains that challenge the clouds,
Gibbons, buffaloes, tigers, elephants,
Ants and all species in this universe

    Are like man's intimate beloved friends
    Companions in the cycle of rebirths
    Priceless existence in time's ageless span
    Radiant treasures of immeasurable worth.

Let others soar beyond the infinite skies
Or tread cosmic paths of moons and stars,
But to this living world my heart is pledged
To Earth bonded in all my lives and deaths.

    I shall even refuse Nirvana
    And suffer the circling wheel of rebirths
    To translate the multitudes of wonders
    Into poems dedicated to this universe.

To cleanse the human world of sorrows
Until peace glows into a golden age;
Then shall my ashes with earth integrate—
A calcified fossil keeping watch.

    If men grew deaf to poetry's charms
    What treasures could replace the loss?
    Even ashes and dust would abhor
    The dryness of the wretched human soul.

If this world were barren of poetry
Then farewell, dear human race,
I would leave to build a realm of the mind
With jewels of rainbow verses.

I shall enchant the celestial realms
With priceless wealth of poetry
My spiritual merits in the arts
Shall outlast time's infinity.

THE DEFIANCE OF A FLOWER

CHIRANAN PITPREECHA

Translated by Sudchit Bhinyoying

W oman has two hands
That hold tight to the substance of life;
Her ply of ligaments is meant of heavy task,
Not for the craving of flimsy silk and damask.

Woman has two feet
To climb the ladder of aspiration,
To strive and stand together,
Not to lean on others.

Woman has eyes
To search for new life
And look far and wide into the world
Not to lure or seduce men.

Woman has a heart
That glows unchangingly,
Amassing all the strength
Because she is complete and human.

Woman has life
That erases errors with reasons.
The value of a free person
Is not to feed the lust of others.

Flowers have sharp thorns,
Not just to blossom and await admirers;
But to bloom and embrace
The fertility of the land.

LIFE

CHIRANAN PITPREECHA

Translated by Chancham Bunnag

The pains burst, probe and pierce.
The nerves throb and twist.
The sweat streams hot and fierce,
Blinding the eyes in blurring mist.
Shadows change, trembling, shift;
Moving lines flee, then meet.
Faint dreams of old days drift
Past the present, winging, fleet,

     To the first sweet phrase . . .
     . . . From the first teetering
     To the brazen preening.
     Twenty-five years living!

Through joy and misery
To be taught by mother.
To be loved by mother.
Blessed more than words can measure.

The pains jerk and shake.
The limbs writhe and flail.
The pangs of birth awake;
The noises wax and wail.

The tiny life from within me
Stirs my life with ecstasy.
Fills me with happy hope,
With daring delight
and dreams of valour . . .
I who am a mother . . .

CHANGE

SAKSIRI MEESOMSUEB

Translated by Chamnongsri L. Rutnin

A clod of earth can burst
  Flung in thunderous explosion
  Foes fall flat right there
Then revived with a mantra

  Wooden guns can kill
  When seen as real
  Slaying throngs of enemy
  Then revived with a magic leaf

Kids gesture anger
In minutes they gesture peace
The bully teases the lil'un
 into tears
Lil'un goes home to Dad
 telling of his hurt
Dad doesn't know
The fake nature of the gun
Dad drills the teaser's ear
With fury and threats
Seizes the wooden gun
 and breaks it,

Not knowing it was but wood
Now the teaser sees it
  as real, real
There, his hands are growing
He sees real guns
            as wooden play-guns
The anger you planted
Has changed the wooden gun
            in his hand

GLOVES

SAKSIRI MEESOMSUEB

Translated by Chamnongsri L. Rutnin

Today, gloved hands touch gloved hands
Hands change gloves change,
Never ever staying the same
Hands in sanitized gloves
Flesh does not feel flesh's warmth
Essence of hands does not mix
And blend with essence of hands
Whatever had happened to human hands
A child's hand is OK. Bare and wondering
It explores as children's hands do
It gropes everywhere it can
Countless piles of garbage
  in which to search
It finds a thrown-away glove
Oh excitement!
At once puts it on
The glove is so easy to take off
Until your hand grows bigger
Then it won't be so easy

CHILD DISHWASHER

SAKSIRI MEESOMSUEB

Translated by Chamnongsri L. Rutnin

'*Kroong kring*' rings spoons on plates
　　Clatters of plates piling on plates
　　Resounding reverberating for miles
Empty used plates are taken out
Loaded new ones are brought in
Eaters who have eaten gradually go out
Eaters who haven't eaten gradually come in
Little leftovers are left on the plates
Gradually piling higher and higher
Until grown terribly big and high
Higher and higher, they're touching the sky
Now they have reached the clouds
Oh, little dishwasher child

　　　Enough food for ten thousand
　　　Hundred thousand, a million years

Moon, oh, dear Moon,
I won't ask you for rice, dear Moon

HIDDEN

SAKSIRI MEESOMSUEB

Translated by Chamnongsri L. Rutnin

Stare, read, rush past, look back
In loud voice she cries, father dear,
It's only ten kilometers to the city

The distant mountain range
Grows big, big, looming near
She hides it with fingers pressed to eyes
So great yet hidden by the fingers

When the mountains come in sight
The Buddha image is then seen
The closer to one city the bigger he becomes
Until the mountain is hidden behind
He sits facing the city
That glimmers below as evening falls

Over the bridge into the city's heart
Great blocks of building tower high
Many cars with so many different faces
Different models, different shapes
Run like busy ants between buildings

. . . All of a sudden Father slams the brakes
Car in front has crashed into another
Squabbling—you're wrong I'm right
Angering, fighting, not stopping to think
Ignoring rules of green yellow red
Car-chaos in a city crazied, Buddha help!
The child murmurs, yes,
Where's the Buddha so majestic and great
That we saw in the distance
Before entering the metropolis
Here in the heart of the city
These great big buildings
Must have hidden him
From the city people's eyes

REAL SILK
FROM MOTHER'S HAND

PHAIWARIN KHAO-NGAM

Translated by B. Kasemsri

Mother grows mulberry to feed worms,
Manual labor of dedication;
She draws silk threads in dreamlike forms
To weave the fabric of her creation.

Every thread's imbued with her spirit,
Maternal embroidery of each cloth;
Her foot repeats the rhythm of heartbeat;
Her hand jerks the bobbin back and forth.

This new piece of shawl to me she gives
With love loomed into every strand;
A life of motherly devotion she lives,
Links her heart to each shimmering band.

I hold up my shawl, mother's gift,
Inter-woven with her precious silk
Her brave soul and moral uplift,
With the blessing of mother's milk.

I can clearly see her delicate hand
That she sometimes used to spank me;
Single-handedly she will withstand
Every danger to defend her son.

> With this hand she builds a lifetime's work,
> With no recompense or relief,
> Then sits at the loom round the clock
> To labor on this silken kerchief.

She has trained her fair daughter
To obey the weaver's behest
And follow her footsteps thereafter;
For mother's weary hands must rest.

> She taught her son to be proud:
> If you love me, she says, ne'er relent,
> Even if they put you in a shroud,
> To fashion free men's covenant.

One day surely I will be gone.
You, children, can continue to weave,
With mother's silk and children's yarn,
So the old cloth can turn a new leaf.

BANANA-LEAF MAIDEN

PHAIWARIN KHAO-NGAM

English translation by B. Kasemsri

My banana-leaf maiden from the plantation,
Used to wrap white rice for provision;
On each field trip or a journey away,
You'd provide rice parcels to last my day.

You offered me rice, when hunger loomed;
Its aroma heartened e'en the mid-day sun;
Each mouthful was fragrantly perfumed
With a light, lasting scent, yet heady one

I had loved you, my banana frond fair,
I once guarded you with a jealous zeal;
Then we parted, with an indifferent air
That no winds of change could conceal.

Lonesome in the age of modernity;
Lonely in the epoch of emptiness;
Lovelorn in the era of frivolity;
Lost in the hour of hopelessness.

I met a giggly polystyrene vamp
At bizarre crossroads; this strange malady,
With the smile of a coquettish tramp,
Lured me to leave my banana lady.

My plantation beauty, cease flapping;
Your green garb will turn grey before long;
When we hear music with plastic wrapping,
'Tis the end of our banana love song.

ABOUT THE AUTHORS

ANCHAN
(Anchalee Vivatanachai)
   Writing has always been her consuming passion even before she came to do it professionally. That, combined with her undeniable talent with words, her wide-ranging imagination, and her perfectionism, helps explain why Anchalee's first published story *Mae Khrap* (Mother Dear) was named the best story of the year by the P.E.N. International Thailand Center in 1985.
   Mae Khrap is one of the 11 stories in the collection entitled *Anyamanee Haeng Chewit* (Jewels of Life), unanimously chosen by the seven-tiered panel of judges for the 1990 S.E.A. Write Award. The panel's statement concerning the winning book may be summarized as follows: "There is a great variety of subject matter in these stories, reflecting a variety of situations and issues inherent in the human condition, some purely personal, some dealing with family or social relationships, others touching on man's eternal quest for life's meaning . . . The language used in each story is eminently suited to its theme and protagonists. The words are selected with an artist's skill and loving care, from those expressing sweet tenderness to those evoking grief, harshness, cruelty, terror . . ."

Anchalee received her secondary education at Rajini Bon School and, in 1974, her bachelor's degree from Chulalongkorn University in Bangkok. In the same year she went to the United States to study at the Gemological Institute of America. Married with a son of eleven, she is now helping her husband in their graphic design company while working for a master's degree in the Teaching of English as a Second Language at City University College in New York.

ANGKARN KALYANAPONG

Born in the southern province of Nakhon Si Thammarat, on February 12, 1926. Angkarn came to Bangkok upon completing his secondary education in his hometown. He enrolled at the Poh Chang School of Fine Arts, and went on to Silpakorn University. Finding the college system and curriculum too confining for his artistic leanings, he left during his junior year and turned his back on the institution.

Poetry has been in his blood. "I was a poet in my previous life," he once declared. One finds poetry in his drawings and writings, even in the characters and spacing in his handwriting. His poems appeared in various magazines and specialized publications during his college days. He struck the reading public with his individual style, deep thoughts, and powerful words. He was honored as the first distinguished contemporary poet by the Sathienkoses-Nagapradipa Foundation in 1972.

By the time he was selected as the S.E.A. Write Awardee for Thailand for the year 1986, Angkarn had become an institution, highly regarded by fellow painters and poets. The award was an overdue honor because his reputation had already transcended the award of any prize, be it official or unofficial. When asked how he felt about the award, he gave a terse reply: "I am not after worldly recognition. My ultimate goal is spiritual liberation."

Angkarn was named Thailand's National Artist in Literature in 1989.

CHIRANAN PITPREECHA

Chiranan Pitpreecha, an advocate of women's rights, was born in 1955 in Trang, a province in southern Thailand. Encouraged by both her mother and her language teacher, she started writing short poems when she was thirteen.

She came to Bangkok to enroll as a science student at Chulalongkorn University and became very involved in the student movement of the time. She was one of the student activists who played a vital role in the October 14, 1973 uprising. She left for the jungles after the political turmoil of October 6, 1976, and returned to Bangkok in 1981.

Later on she went to study for an advanced degree in history at Cornell University. She is now back in Thailand, writing poetry and working on her Ph.D dissertation. Her collection of poems titled *The Lost Leaf* won the S.E.A. Write Award in 1989. She is married to Seksan Prasertkul, a former student leader.

KHOMTHUAN KHANTHANU

(Prasartphorn Bhususilpthorn)

Thailand's fifth S.E.A. Write Awardee is known to Thai readers as the poet Khomthuan Khanthanu, but his real name is Prasartphorn Bhususilpthorn. He was born in Thonburi Province in 1950. Prasartphorn finished his secondary education at the Suan Kularb Boys' School and enrolled in Thammasart University studying journalism. His original love of poetry, combined with his journalistic skill, pushed him into the front row during the events leading to the October 14, 1973 student uprising. Years later, in 1976, his poems appeared in magazines. The name Khomthuan Khanthanu is used for poetical works, and Kosum Phisai for short stories. They are known and loved for their harsh and sarcastic tones. His associates named him the "Iron Poet".

Since 1979, Prasartphorn took up writing as his career, working as a full-time columnist. He has had many books published as collections of short stories and poems, such as *Saeng Dao Haeng Sattha* (The Star of Faith), *Samnuk Kabot* (Conscience of a Rebel), *Nattakam Bon Lan Kwang* (Drama on An Open Space) and *Khon*

Tok Ngan (The Jobless). The collection of poems, *Nattakam Bon Lan Kwang*, won him the S.E.A. Write Award for 1983.

NAOWARAT PONGPAIBOON

Naowarat was born on March 26, 1939 in Phanom Thuan District in the western province of Kanchanaburi, where he remained until he finished his secondary schooling. He came to Bangkok at pre-university level and went to read law at Thammasat University where he graduated in 1965.

After graduation, Naowarat entered the monkhood during which he journeyed south to study Buddhism with the renowned Buddhadasa Bhikkhu of Surat Thani Province. After a brief interlude of two years as a publisher and one year as a lecturer, Naowarat joined the Bangkok Bank, Ltd. in 1973, first as a public relations officer and later as the director of the bank's Music and Drama Center, a post which he still holds.

Meanwhile, Naowarat has been writing both prose and poetry which appear regularly in newspapers and magazines. A keen flutist, Naowarat transposes melifluous music to his poems. He is a naturalist at heart. Buddhist and Zen doctrines also play important parts in his poetry. He won the coveted S.E.A. Write Award in 1980 and was named Thailand's National Artist in 1993.

PHAITHUN THANYA

(Thanya Sangkapanthanon)

Phaithun Thanya, the 1987 S.E.A. Write awardee, was born in Patthalung, a district in southern Thailand, received his education in the south, and graduated from Songkhla Teachers College. At present he teaches at a small secondary school in a small district in Sukhothai, an ancient capital of the kingdom. He has recently acquired a masters degree from Si Nakharinwirot University and plans to go on teaching and writing as before. "Teaching is my profession," he says, "writing has always been my dream and aspiration."

His winning work, *Ko Kong Sai* (Building Sandpiles), a collection of twelve short stories, was published in 1985. This was the first time Phaithun Thanya's writing appeared in book form.

PHAIWARIN KHAO-NGAM

Phaiwarin Khao-ngam comes from a farming family in Roi Et, northeast Thailand. His education included training as a novice, then a monk, in a Buddhist college for the Sangha and as a teacher there in language and Thai literature. Upon leaving the monkhood, he started work in journalism, first as a proofreader, then as a reporter for a local newspaper in the northern city of Chiang Mai. He came to Bangkok in 1985, working for a number of journals and magazines before joining *Siam Rath* daily where he is at present in the editorial department. He remains, however, a freelance writer first and foremost.

The first collection of his poems was published in 1985. Four more followed, earning him acclaim from his fellow poets and readers. He was expected to win the S.E.A. Write Award in the future.

The Banana-Stem Horse, which was selected for the 1995 S.E.A. Write Award was also published this year.

For those who have not seen a banana-stem horse, this is a traditional popular toy made from banana stem. A child might be seen riding on it around the house or in a playground, sometimes carrying a banana-stem gun and pretending to be a hero fighting an enemy.

SAKSIRI MEESOMSUEB
(Kittisak Meesomsueb)

Saksiri's winning work, a book of poetry, whose rhythm combines the classical and the innovative, is entitled *Those Hands Are White*.

"I think children's hands are the whitest of all," he said in a recent interview.

He is a teacher of art and music in a district school in Nakorn Sawan, his native city. A graduate of Poh Chang Art School in Bangkok, he says his thinking and feeling have also been influenced by the extra-curricular education given by his parents and relatives, and by the monks he served when he was a monastery boy. He would also like everyone to know that his spiritual father is the late Chang Sae Tang, a well-known Thai poet.

Innocence, simplicity, lack of malice, compassion—such qualities impress and inspire him. His poems, as expressed by the judging committee, bring hope to the reader that this world of ours may attain peace and beauty through goodness of heart.

Of the S.E.A. Write Award or any awards, Saksiri says: "I always tell my students entering contests that awards come and go, but if we have creativity, and it stays with us, that is an award in itself."

SILA KHOMCHAI
(Winai Boonchuay)

Sila Khomchai's award-winning work is a collection of thirteen short stories entitled *Khropkhrua Klang Thanon* (Mid-road Family).

In the foreword to the collection, Sila has this to say about short story writing:

"In the country no one can earn a living by writing short stories. They are created in spare time, time which is snatched from time meant for relaxation after a long day's work, time so very vital to people living in a big city who come home exhausted by the pressures of work, by the agonizing reality of traveling to work, of getting on buses, of breathing in the polluted air . . ."

Sila goes on to say that one has to love doing it. Sometimes one has to squeeze oneself to the utmost for the energy to do it, and sometimes one does it even when it is painful.

The stories mostly deal with middle-class people meeting the manifold challenges of big-city living, of the yearnings and disappointments and dreams, of strength and weakness, cruelty and kindness, all portrayed in a language at once both realistic and lyrical.

Sila Khomchai comes from southern Thailand, attended Ramkhamhaeng University, was a student activist in the 1970s, and was in the jungle living an ideological-oriented life for a number of years before returning to live in Bangkok. He is now a pragmatic journalist who has never lost his humanitarian ideals.

USSIRI THAMMACHOT

The third S.E.A. Write awardee for Thailand was born in Hua-Hin District, Prachuap Khiri Khan Province on July 10, 1947, the youngest child in a fisherman's family. He studied at the Klai-kangwon School in his district, and left for Bangkok before completing his secondary education. He first sat for the university entrance examination in 1967, but failed to get a place to study political science. His family, in the meantime, ran into financial trouble. Ussiri decided to find a job as an employee of the National Statistics Office. He did surveys in the northeast for two years, gaining invaluable experience.

Ussiri returned to his studies when he successfully enrolled in the Faculty of Mass Communications of Chulalongkorn University. He started writing short stories. His first published story won the award of the university's Literary Club. He also ventured into the magazine business, producing a number of movie magazines, all well-known and popular, but finally not viable.

After his graduation, Ussiri joined the publishing business concentrating on magazines and newspapers. He is currently with the *Siam Rath* newspaper. He handles news, articles, and short stories. His short stories use themes from his childhood days near the sea and experiences gained from rural life in the northeast written in strong and terse language. His has been dubbed "prose poetry". His first collection of short stories *Khunthong, You Will Return at Dawn* won him the S.E.A. Write Award for 1981, making him the third Thai awardee.

VANICH CHARUNGKIJ-ANANT

Born on August 9, 1948, in Suphan Buri Province, Vanich received his education in his hometown, and went to Bangkok to study at the School of Fine Arts. He later pursued his art studies at the Faculty of Painting, Sculpture and Prints, Silpakorn University, where he graduated with a Bachelor of Arts degree. Subsequently, he went to the United States to further his study and earned a master's degree in Fine Arts.

Vanich took up writing before his college days, concentrating on poems. The rich heritage of folk music in Suphan Buri, his home town, serves as a solid base for his artistic and literary endeavors. He became famous among college readers, with his linguistic skill and great sense of humor. His first short story was published in *Lalana* magazine in 1972. Three years later he began writing a regular series, *Chotmai Thung Phuan* (Letters to Friends.)

Vanich worked briefly with a magazine and a commercial bank, before furthering his studies in the United States. On his return to Thailand, he took up a job with a publishing house, and became a freelance writer and columnist afterwards. He is now fully occupied with writing assignments which also include songs and television scripts. He has many collections of short stories, poems, features, and children's stories to his credit. His collection of short stories, *Soi Dieo Kan* (Down the Same Lane) won him the prestigious S.E.A. Write Award for 1984.

S.E.A. WRITE AWARD-WINNING THAI SHORT STORY AND POETRY COLLECTIONS

(Note that the award is given each year to only one of the three genres—poems, short stories, and novels—on a rotating basis. Those selections included in this anthology are listed after the collection titles.)

1980
Poetry
 Mere Movement (Phiang Khwam Khruan Wai)
 Naowarat Pongpaiboon
  Mere Movement
  The Way of the Snail

1981
Short Stories
 Khunthong, You Will Return at Dawn
 (Khunthong Chao Cha Klap Mua Fa Sang)
 Ussiri Thammachot
  Nightfall on the Waterway
  On the Route of the Rabid Dog

1993
Poetry

> *Drama on a Wide Arena (Nattakam Bon Lan Kwang)*
> Khomthuan Khanthanu
>> *A Beggar's Chant*

1984
Short Stories

> *Down the Same Lane (Soi Dieo Kan)*
> Vanich Charungkij-anant
>> *The Barter*
>> *The Song of the Leaves*

1986
Poetry

> *A Poet's Pledge (Panithan Kawi)*
> Angkarn Kalayanapong
>> *A Poet's Pledge*

1987
Short Stories

> *Building Sandpiles (Ko Kong Sai)*
> Phaithun Thanya
>> *People on the Bridge*
>> *The Prophecy*

1989
Poetry

> *The Lost Leaf (Bai Mai Thi Hai Pai)*
> Chiranan Pitpreecha
>> *The Defiance of a Flower*
>> *Life*

1992
Poetry
>*Those Hands are White (Mu Nun Si Khao)*
>Saksiri Meesomsueb
>>*Change*
>>*Child Dishwasher*
>>*Gloves*
>>*Hidden*

1993
Short Stories
>*Mid-road Family (Khrop Khrua Klang Thanon)*
>Sila Khomchai
>>*Mid-road Family*
>>*"Sawdust Brain" and the Wrapping Paper*

1995
Poetry
>*The Banana-Stem Horse (Ma Kan Kluai)*
>Phaiwarin Khao-ngam
>>*Banana-Leaf Maiden*
>>*Real Silk from Mother's Hand*